SOMETIMES IT MAKES YOU WONDER

DR. RICHARD ORZECK

Purrfect Love Publishing
Trumansburg, New York 14886

Purrfect Love Publishing
PO Box 655
Trumansburg, New York 14886
(607) 387-3490

Printed in the U.S.A.

10 9 8 7 6 5 4 3 2 1
First Edition

ISBN: 0-9704275-3-0 (perfect bound)
       0-9704275-4-9 (case bound)

With love and infinite gratitude, I dedicate this
humble book to all of the great teachers who helped
make my dream of becoming a vet come true.

INTRODUCTION

Every occupation or field of study has its legendary superstars. They are the men and women who have excelled, who have risen to the top of their various professions. They set the standards by which all who follow afterwards are judged. The game of football has Coach Vince Lombardi, modern day science has Albert Einstein, the realm of politics has Jesse "the Body" Ventura, Hollywood has Arnold Schwarzenegger and Marilyn Monroe, and pop music has Madonna. In the world of veterinary medicine, we have the great Dr. Francis H. Fox.

For over sixty years, Professor Fox has been hard at work successfully accomplishing one of the most arduous jobs a person could possibly be expected to do: that of teaching aspiring students the noble profession of veterinary medicine. Although his main skills as a veterinarian are in caring for and treating large animals (cows, pigs, and horses), his teaching specialty is that of the fine art of physical diagnosis.

(Dr. Fox, the generous and unpretentious man that he is, insisted that I inform the readers of this book that any benefits of physical diagnosis a vet student of his may have acquired from his instruction were taught to him way back in the dark ages of his unruly youth by *his* teacher, the late Dr. Walter J. Gibbons.)

Physical diagnosis is the medical ability to determine disease using only four of the five physical senses: seeing, feeling, hearing, and smelling. (Regardless of a doctor's dedication, it is not all that prudent to taste any aspect of their patients or their diseases.) Prior to our age of computers and modern diagnostic equipment—CAT scans, MRIs, ultrasound machines, etc.—veterinarians and physicians since the time of Hippocrates have had to depend on our skills of physical diagnosis to help heal and save the lives of our patients. In Dr. Fox's lectures, we learned to understand and nurture the healing touch of laying on our hands, of the important need to smell our patient's breath and body fluids, of carefully and systematically listening to our patient's hearts and viscera, and of seeing what only a well-trained eye can detect in the abnormality of a patient's gait or the subtle color change of an animal's gums.

But it was not just his mastery of instructing physical diagnosis that kept us anxious students captivated by his lectures; it was also his colorful ability to share the valuable personal experiences and observations he has amassed from his sixty-plus years of stomping out disease that kept us all ears. Even though he presided over his classes with the tenderness and grace of a Marine Corps drill sergeant with a bad toothache, he was every once in a while prone to prolonged and often sensitive moments of nostalgic reflection.

These insights into the real world of veterinary medicine would cover every possible subject from valuable safety tips like "Don't put your hand in a pig's mouth" to practical advice on pet ownership: "I had three cats in my life that, for some reason, vomited all of the time. One of them used to eat it back up as soon as she was done. I liked her the best."

One of his most memorable stories was about an experience he'd had while trying to examine a milk cow. The man who called him to the farm was a little concerned that the cow wasn't eating as well as she should. Dr. Fox told us that he could find absolutely nothing wrong with the cow except an inability to find the critter's heartbeat. (Finding a heartbeat in a cow is usually quite simple because they have such enormous hearts.) He then continued on for a long time telling us how he tried all of the old tricks he knew to find—in his words—"the damned heartbeat," but was unsuccessful with any of them. Technically, he concluded, the old girl should not have been alive.

And this was the point he was trying to get across to us eager vet students. "Sometimes," he said, "despite all of your knowledge and best efforts, you have to just stand back and wonder what in the heck [heck was not the exact word he used] is going on."

This story had quite a profound effect on me; to this very day, it still gives me great comfort. I remember thinking at the time that if a great healer like Dr. Fox can still be periodically baffled and mystified by this business of veterinary medicine—especially after being at it since the time of Moses—then I, too, should have no problem.

I hope this book will share some of the wonders I've experienced over my humble last ten years as a veterinarian: the good, the ugly, the awe-inspiring, the frustrating, and, of course, the bizarre. Thankyou.

Contents

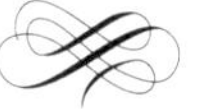

CHAPTER ONE

THE BIG BUFFALO ROUNDUP

People are always asking me, "Doc, what's the most interesting case you've ever had to work on?" My usual answer to this not-so-easy question is that just about every problem I've had to deal with in my veterinary career is interesting. We veterinarians are quite lucky in that we get a double bonus with each of our patient interactions: We get to hear both the story of the pet (the patient) as well as that of the client (the pet's owner). And believe me, its amazing the number of interesting stories I've heard in this business. However, if someone were to press me *really* hard to tell them what I thought was the most extraordinary case I've ever been called on to handle, it would have to be the time I had the honor to meet the late Mr. Shenandoah and to help him to round up his magnificent herd of buffalo.

That day had started out simple enough. It was in the autumn of my last year of vet school, and I was doing my first rotation through ambulatory medicine. The ambulatory medicine rotation is the segment of our veterinary training where we get to go out into the countryside to visit farms and get hands-on experience in treating large animals. While on these farm calls, we would get to do everything from helping a dairy cow deliver her baby calf to trimming the hooves of a llama; from castrating baby piglets to floating the teeth of giant draft horses. With the exception of just a couple of my big-city classmates, the two-week sessions spent doing ambulatory medicine were everyone's favorite.

One of the big events that occurred in our upstate New York region during that autumn was the escape of a herd of buffalo from the Onondaga Indian Reservation. The giant beasts were making the headlines of the local papers every single day. Most of the stories were figments of reporters' imaginations, and even the stories that were true were usually exaggerated for effect. The poor critters were allegedly creating traffic problems on the interstate highway that ran through the reservation, were trashing apple orchards, upsetting high school football games, and plundering Christmas tree plantations. One thing was certain, however: local non—Native American landowners were getting upset. Tempers were flaring, and it was feared that before long, one of these magnificent animals would be shot.

Rumors had been circulating around my vet school for several days that a big roundup was soon going to occur, and that our veterinary expertise would be needed when the situation demanded it. The first time I suspected that I was going to be involved was during the daily routine lunchtime briefing. The professor in charge of my rotation suddenly, just out of the blue, asked me if I knew how to fire a rifle. "Of course," I answered, a little bit surprised by the question. "What's going on?"

It was a strange question to ask me, because I'm sure that he had to know the answer before he even asked me the question. From all of the small talk we'd had riding around the countryside on our way to farm calls, the man knew I'd been raised on a farm and that I'd also been in the military. But before I could get in another word, he told our group he had to make a quick phone call and that he'd be right back.

A few minutes later, he returned from the receptionist's office and filled us all in on what was going on. "The buffalo have finally all been rounded up," he said. "They're in a small pasture about five miles from the reservation. The county sheriff has called and has asked for our help. I've told them we'd be right up there as soon as we could."

He then spent the next ten minutes presenting us with the rough details of his plan. I sat there patiently and waited until everyone else finished speaking—after all, I was just a lowly student—before asking him the question foremost on my mind: "Professor, why did you ask me if I could fire rifle?" I was just a little bit nervous that I might be asked to shoot one or more of these buffalo, which I'd made up my mind to absolutely not do.

His answer brought me great relief. "Tranquilizer rifle is what I meant to say." He then added, "Richard, would you have any problem if you had to fire from a helicopter?" I told him that would be no problem at all. After much discussion, it was decided that one intern, two senior residents, and I, would head up to the roundup and see what we could do to help.

I was assigned to ride along with a young veterinarian from South Africa, who was doing an internship in large animal medicine at my university. I'd ridden with Dr. Peter previously on several other occasions and found him quite easy to get along with. One of the things I remember most about him was that he was endlessly astounded—overwhelmed might be a better way to put it—with our rural American culture. The simple act of stopping at a rural lunchroom or diner was a major cultural event for him. One time, another classmate and I treated him at a local A&W restaurant to a chili dog with cheese and a root beer float. The encounter filled him with gustatory ecstasy. He was a good kid, and I was glad I was going to ride with him.

A second truck would be driven by the two senior residents. These guys would have the tranquilizer and the tranquilizer rifles. They would also tow a trailer with two horses and their riding gear. As the professor gave us our instructions, I could see the look of delight on Dr. Peter's face when he heard there would be horses involved. I'm positive that visions of cowboys and buffalo and the Wild West all danced in his young, fertile mind. Likewise, in all fairness to him, I'd be lying if I told anyone that I wasn't a little bit excited about the new adventure myself.

And so, after loading up, we drove off ; not into the sunset, but northward toward the reservation. It was a perfect afternoon for a ride. The two residents drove in front of us pulling the horse trailer, and Dr. Peter and I followed. Being familiar with the area, I knew it would take us an hour or so to drive up to the reservation, so I just kicked back to enjoy the ride. And what a ride it was! The day could not have been more perfect. All the farmers up and down the valley were out taking full advantage of the nice weather to get in the their harvests, everywhere there were black-and-white Holstein dairy cows out in the pastures contently grazing on the last of the season's green grass, and the fall foliage was at its peak of perfection. More than one time, I happened to look over toward Dr. Peter. Without him having to say a single word, I could tell by the wide-eyed look on his face that he, too, was marveling at the magnificence of the moment.

About an hour and a half later (we'd made a quick stop for coffee), we arrived at one of the local firehouses that had been set up as the command post for the big roundup. The parking lot was filled to capacity with sheriffs' cars, state police cruisers, ambulances, and TV network communications vans; the whole thing looked like a war zone. We were thanked for showing up and then given directions to the field where the buffalo were being temporarily confined.

When we arrived at the pasture, the first thing I noticed was the large number of pickup trucks and horse trailers. Somehow or other, the word had gotten out that there was going to be a roundup, and there had to be fifty or more horses with their riders. What made it even more interesting was that these riders were of every persuasion and skill level you could imagine, from silver-spurred, city-slicker, Wyatt Earp wanna-bes, all the way up to professional, uniformed, mounted law enforcement officers. There even appeared to be a couple of genuine cowboys in the lot.

Dr. Peter and I, after surveying and analyzing the whole situation, decided to walk down to the corral and actually get a close-up look at the buffalo. They were a small group of about twenty adult animals along with four or five calves. All of them were lying down in the warm afternoon sun, peacefully chewing their cud and resting. Standing off by themselves were two Native American—looking men eating bologna sandwiches. My first thought was that they were the animals' owners.

Because I was curious, I walked up to them and stood next to them for a couple of minutes and just looked at the buffalo. One of the men was younger looking, quite stout, who had on a worn-out, black straw cowboy hat, a red checkered flannel work shirt, a big turquoise belt buckle, and a new-looking pair of blue jeans. The other man was shorter in height. His long, straight, charcoal gray hair made him look quite a bit older; his face was weathered and tanned; he reminded me of a picture I'd once seen of an old biblical patriarch. He wore a white T-shirt, worn blue jeans, and had on a brown pair of cowboy boots. I was later told that these two men were father and son. After standing there for a couple of seconds, I turned to the two of them and said hello. The father turned toward me, and after he finished chewing and swallowing his mouthful of sandwich, he nodded his head and replied, "Afternoon, son," and then he turned back to look at the buffalo.

After a couple more minutes I again broke the silence. "These guys belong to you?" I asked.

Without looking away from the herd, the older man answered, "Yup."

Not wanting to disturb their obviously deep concentration any further, I waited a couple of minutes before expressing to them a couple of my own thoughts on the whole situation. "Ya know, sir, my wife and I have a herd of beef cows. Occasionally, the little darlings misbehave and break out of their pasture. When that happens, all my wife has to do is get a bucket of grain, walk out onto the field, and they'll usually follow her home." As I pointed to the giant critters in front of us, I asked, "Do you think it might just work the same with these guys?"

Both men turned and stared at me with a look of profound disbelief on their faces. A slight feeling of foreboding suddenly came over me as I stood there wondering what I'd just said wrong. As I write these words today and think back to that exact moment, it's my humble opinion that if the older man had been a little younger and perhaps less worldly and experienced in the weaknesses of his fellow humans, he might just have snapped back at me with a scathing reply, maybe something to the effect of: "Young man, are you mentally impaired in some way? Don't you know that these buffalo are wild animals who could, if they put their minds to it, crush you like a bug?" Or even worse, he might have just flat out told me what a moron he thought I was.

But no, after a couple of seconds, the look on his old and tired face changed from that of disbelief to one of loving and patient understanding; he knew I was just a simple pilgrim trying to find my way in this enormous world where there is always so, so much to know. He smiled and said, "No, son, that trick doesn't work with buffalo, they're not as docile as cattle are." He then turned back to watching his buffalo and finishing his bologna sandwich.

I could see he was in deep thought, so I didn't bother him again. I just stood there watching him as he watched his animals. As a matter of fact, everyone, from the cops to the cowboys, all just stood there, waiting for something to happen. Every now and again, a horse would snort or an impatient grumbling would arise from one of the onlookers, but mostly, everyone just waited. And waited. And waited.

Suddenly, without any warning, the old man turned to his son and spoke some words that I didn't understand. He then turned back to his resting buffalo and firmly spoke some more words that I, again, didn't understand. As soon as he finished, he turned to me and everyone standing in our vicinity and shouted, "They're ready to go home. Please, folks, I want you all to give them lots of room." He and his son then walked over to the pasture gate, cleared a wide path in the crowd, and waited for his animals to rouse.

It wasn't long before one enormous male buffalo sprang to his feet. As he stood, he violently shook off the stiffness in his limbs and back, and with the calm assurance of being the big boss, he then started walking around his herd mates, getting them up and ready for their big journey back home.

When they were all standing, the old man spoke to them one more time in his mysterious language. I imagined what he said to them was something like, "Have a safe journey, you guys," or perhaps, "Come on, you guys, go straight home and please, please, please don't stop to eat any Christmas trees on the way." He then opened the gate, and out they thundered. The critters quickly made their way onto the dirt road, turned left, and headed west toward their reservation home.

By the time I got to the road myself, all I could see was dust and bouncing buffalo butts; these guys were moving! And about this same time, like they'd been waiting their whole lives to do so, all of the yippee-ki-yi, whoop-de-do, cowboy wanna-bes mounted their anxious horses and went chasing down the road after them. Right on these yahoos' tails were police cruisers, network news vans, and about a hundred screaming cars and pickup trucks. You just had to wonder what was going on in all of these folks' heads.

Before I go any further, in the hope of not sounding too self-righteous about the whole situation, I must make two sad confessions: The first (and I'm slightly embarrassed to say this) is that my two resident colleagues—who should have known better—mounted their horses and joined this episode of mass stupidity. Secondly, I, too, ran along in hot pursuit. But only for about ten seconds, because even though I'd not had all that much experience in my life with chasing buffalo (I'd actually had none), it didn't take me long to realize that running after these giant creatures, either on horse or by foot, was a pretty asinine thing to do. And so I stopped and said to myself, "Richard, what in the heck are you doing? You might just as well wait here till everyone gets back."

So I did. But as I stood there alone by the side of the road, catching my breath—with all expectations of having a thrilling helicopter ride now just a distant memory—and wondering how the heck I'd ended up on this dirt road in the middle of the boonies in the first place (even Dr. Peter had disappeared in the mass of humanity), this old, rusted-out, yellowish Toyota pickup truck pulled up alongside me. In the cab were the father and son who I'd had the short conversation with moments earlier. The son, who was driving, hollered out the window, "Wanna go for a ride with us?"

Having nothing better to do, I said, "Sure," and then I hopped into the back of the truck. In a second, we were off. The son then followed the chaotic mass for about a half mile. At this point, the big roundup bore sharply to the right in order to circle around the base of a large mountain. To my surprise—along with a slight bit of uneasiness—the son, rather than continuing to follow the pack, instead drove straight ahead onto another dirt road. This road (it was more like a cowpath) zigged and zagged up and up and up and finally brought us to the very top of the hill, where we then parked in the middle of a field of corn stubble.

What a beautiful view we all had from the top of this mountain; I mean, it was like you could see the whole of the countryside around us. As a general rule, I'm not one to ponder such things at any length, but the glory of it all was overwhelming. We got out of the truck, and after a couple of minutes of taking it all in, we located the drama of the big buffalo roundup as it continued to play itself out down in the valley below.

From our high vantage point, we could watch the buffalo and their entire escort plow their way through fields, forests, creeks, and roadways. First, they'd run this way and then that way, and then back this way and then that way again; it looked to me like they were all hopelessly lost. Although, at first, I said nothing to my new friends, I was a little worried that the law enforcement officers were soon

•

going to lose their patience with these lumbering beasts and might just begin shooting them.

When I finally got up enough nerve to mention my concerns to the old man and his son, neither said a word. It seemed as if they were, again, in deep thought, and I don't think they heard me; so I said no more and just stood there and waited. After a couple more minutes of this silence, the strangest thing began to happen. As a matter of fact, it was so amazing that if I hadn't seen it with my own eyes, I would never, in a million years, have believed it.

The old man, again in a language I didn't understand, started speaking in a half-chanting, half-talking voice. As soon as he spoke, his herd of buffalo, way down in the valley below, stopped moving. It was unbelievable! It was like an invisible giant hand had appeared before them, telling them to stop. Then, after giving his animals a few minutes to catch their breath, the old man, in English this time, said, "OK, my children, just relax. Take it easy and don't be afraid. I'm up here on the hill watching you. When you're ready, just start walking in the direction of the setting sun." And they did! "OK, now turn left around that fence."

As he spoke, the herd responded to his every word. After each set of commands, the father and son discussed with each other what would be the best route for the herd to follow. These directions would then be relayed by the father to their buffalo. I just stood there in awe. They continued to guide the buffalo for about fifteen minutes until they were at last out of sight around the back of another mountain. The father's final direction to them was that they turn neither right nor left but just keep moving straight ahead. He finished by telling them he'd meet them all at the other side of the mountain.

No sooner had he finished speaking than, in a flash, we were back in the old Toyota and barreling down the hill. When we reached the bottom, rather than turning in the direction the buffalo had been traveling, we circled in the other direction around the base of the mountain. After driving several miles, we turned right onto a blacktopped valley road. After a couple of miles, the son slowed the old pickup down to a crawl. As we drove along, the old man, from the passenger seat, stared with all his might into the thick woods lining the right side of the road. Without warning, he hollered across the cab to his son, "Stop here; this is where they're gonna come down." And so the son stopped, backed up about twenty feet, and pulled the truck off to the side of the road.

We then all got out and walked over to where the father decided the buffalo were going to appear. Again, I was a little confused. The thick brush and trees at the spot where he thought the buffalo were going to come down the mountain looked to me like the same thick trees and brush that we'd seen lining the road for the past mile. Quite perplexed, I couldn't stop myself from asking, "Sir, this all looks the same to me; I mean, there's no trail, no pathway, no nothing! How do you know they're going to come down the mountain at this exact spot?"

The old man again just looked at me and smiled. He had in his countenance that same look of compassionate understanding he'd shown me earlier back at the corral; again, he knew I was just a pilgrim. He said, "Son, the reason I know this is the spot is because it's where I *told* them to come out." And that was that, and I said no more.

After a few more minutes of strategy planning between the old man and his son, the father turned to me and asked whether I'd be interested in helping them. Without a second of hesitation, I told him it would be my honor to do so. The slight smile on his face told me he was pleased by my willingness to help. "Good," he said, "let's go then," and we all set out walking about a quarter mile farther down the road. When we reached the spot he felt was just right (and again, it looked no different to me from any other spot) he turned to me and said, "OK, son, I want you to stand right here."

Being an agreeable kind of guy, I said, "No problem, sir. What do you think's going to happen?"

Pointing back up the road to where we had left the truck, he said, "When the buffalo come out of the woods up there, my son and I will tell them to head down the road toward you." He then pointed his arm westward up the steep hill to my right. "When they come running down the road and get close to where you're standing, I want you to point in that direction and tell them that's where they have to go."

It was a couple of seconds before the initial shock of what he just said had passed, and I could finally speak. "Sir," I said, the concern in my voice probably obvious, "let me make sure I have this straight. You want me to stand here in the middle of the road, as a herd of scared, tired, and confused buffalo race toward me. Then, as they get close to me, you want me to point and tell them to turn and go that way up the hill? If you don't mind me asking, how can I be sure they'll listen to what I say and not trample me to death?"

He looked at me as I looked back at him, and with the calmness and assurance of someone who has lived a long life, he said, "Son, don't worry. When they come down from the hill up the road there where I'll be standing, I'll make sure to tell them to do exactly what you say." With that, having no more to say, he and his son walked back up the road to their pickup.

As I stood there alone along the side of another country back road, I found myself, for the second time that day, wondering what in the heck I was doing. Somehow or other, through no great effort of my own, I was now even more out in the boonies than I was before. Additionally, I was now stuck with the job of potentially having to play traffic cop for a herd of charging buffalo. To make matters worse—at least in my own frenzied little mind—there was no one (just in case something went wrong), except the old man and his son, who knew where I was. So, again, not quite knowing what else to do, I did nothing.

Time passed very slowly on that country road; fifteen minutes slipped by, then a half hour, then one hour, and then two. Once in a while, from way up on the mountain to my left, I could hear the occasional shout or scream of one of the Wild West yahoos harassing those poor and tired buffalo. In my mind's eye, I imagined seeing one or more of those same ignorant greenhorns being trampled and eviscerated by those same frustrated buffalo.

But after some time, the distant hollers were eventually drowned out by a state police helicopter. I wasn't quite sure what was going on, but all I could think of was that some poor slob was probably getting air evacuated out because of some senseless injury. And all the while as I waited, I practiced with myself exactly what I was going to tell the buffalo. Although I wouldn't admit it to myself at the time, I was also rehearsing in my mind (just in case) what I would do if these charging buffalo didn't listen to me when I told them to turn.

After two hours had passed, I saw another small pickup truck stop by the old man and his son. The driver, a lady, after talking with them for a short time, handed something to the father. She then drove down to where I was posted. The woman turned out to be the old man's daughter-in-law, and she was bringing me a much-welcome bologna and cheese sandwich and a can of Coke. After handing them to me, she kindly filled me in on what was happening.

From what she'd heard on the CB radio and police scanner, it turned out that the helicopter that I had seen flying around over the top of the mountain was not keeping an eye on the buffalo or evacuating wounded, but rather it was there to help out the cowboys themselves. It so happened that in their excitement of the big chase, the good old boys had gotten themselves lost. The helicopter had been called in to help the mighty warriors find their way back to their pickups. I couldn't resist the smile that came onto my face when she told me this.

I then asked her where the buffalo were. She said she wasn't sure because, according to the scanner, they'd disappeared into the woods about a half hour ago and could no longer be spotted from the air. After spending a couple more minutes talking about the weather, the buffalo, and how I liked vet school, she turned her truck around and drove back up the road from where she had come.

It wasn't five minutes later, just as I was taking the last bite of my sandwich, that I saw the old man and his son quickly move from the side of the road, where they'd been standing next to their pickup truck, to the center. A quick second later, the old man started waving his arms up and down, making sure he had my attention. I waved back, and he then hollered down to me, "Here they come! Get ready!"

No sooner did he finish talking than from out of the woods and onto the center of the road scrambled the large male leader of the pack. He spun around several times, like he was confused, and then just stood there, pawing the asphalt with his massive left front foot. In about another ten seconds, the entire herd was out of the woods and standing on the road next to him. After a few more seconds of trying to get their bearings, they grouped up and began moving in my direction. It was now going to be up to me to stand my ground and direct these mad, confused, and homesick critters back toward their reservation.

And I have to admit that I was scared poopless. "Richard," I said to myself, "what in the heck [heck was not the word I used] are you doing? Don't you know these guys can kill you? Run! Get out of the way!" But I didn't move. Somehow, somewhere, in the deepest recesses of my terrified little brain, I'd decided that I had absolute confidence in the instructions and advice of the old man. So I just stood there, like the Rock of Gibraltar, as the beasts thundered toward me.

When the lead bull got about thirty feet away from where I was standing, I pointed with both hands toward the right. At the same time, in a fearless though somewhat shaky voice, I shouted, "Go that way, you guys; your daddy wants you to go up that there hill." Then I closed my eyes and waited for the impact.

But the impact never came. I opened my eyes for a second, and there was the leader, stopped in front of me, just looking at me; it was like he wanted me to tell him again just what to do. When I look back at that fateful moment on that lonely country back road, what amazes me the most is that once he and I made eye contact, I felt not one bit of fear. As that magnificent creature stood there, steam gushing forth from his gigantic flared nostrils, so exhausted from the journey that he could barely stand, all I could feel for him was overwhelming compassion. Also sadness; sadness for the way his kind had been mercilessly slaughtered to near extinction in the last century at the hands of men like those now pathetically lost up on the hilltop.

After a couple of seconds of staring into the eye of the beast, the reality of the situation returned to me, and, not knowing what else to do, I continued pointing toward the hill to the right and once more said, "Your daddy told me to tell you all to please go this way." The lead bull, apparently understanding what I'd just said, shook his head, snorted the most god-awful sound you'd ever want to hear, and then turned to his left. Without a moment of hesitation, he charged headlong through the bushes lining the road and continued running up the mountain through the trees. The herd immediately followed his lead, and in about a minute, they were out of sight. Needless to say, I was quite relieved.

After the last buffalo had left the road, I saw the old man and his son get in their pickup and drive down the road toward me. They parked along the road next to where the animals had just disappeared. The father quickly got out of the truck and then began studying the trail. I watched him silently as he did so. After about a minute, he hollered into the passenger-side window to his son, "OK, I'll see ya up top." The son then drove away.

Without giving me a chance to answer either yes or no, the father told me to follow him. And, again, not knowing what else to do, I did. Up and up the hill we ran, through black raspberry bushes and thorn apples, up the buffalo's trail through the woods. It had to have been nearly a mile straight up. I had all I could do to keep up with the old man; he climbed the rocks, scrambled over fallen trees, and jumped across small ravines like he was a young white-tailed deer. It was incredible.

When we reached the top of the hill, we came upon a section of barbed wire fence that was the boundary for the buffalo's pasture. It was here that we discovered the reason why the critters had originally escaped. Some creep had purposely cut all of the wires. This didn't go over well with the old man. "Why do they gotta do this to us all of the time?" he lamented over and over, "Why don't they just leave us alone?"

He and I then spent the next several minutes attempting a temporary repair of the fence. As the old man tried his best to attach the cut ends of the strands of barbed wire together, I searched about for some large branches that could be placed in front of the hole until a permanent repair could be made. When he was satisfied the repair was enough to hold his buffalo in for a while, we started walking across the huge pasture to where his son would be waiting for us.

And as we walked, he and I talked all about his beloved buffalo. He told me the history of the herd and how important they were to the traditions of his people. Knowing I was a beef farmer as well as a veterinarian (I'd told him over and over again that I was only still just a veterinary student, but it didn't seem to matter to him), we talked about some of the medical aspects of his herd as well. He expressed to me his concern that about only half of his females had managed to give birth during the previous couple of calving seasons. Likewise, he was worried that the calves that had been born earlier in the spring were not growing as well as he felt they should.

I had some ideas and opinions on what might be the cause of his problems, and he was anxious to hear every word I had to say. As a matter of fact, he was so eager to hear what I had to say, he suggested that maybe we stop and sit for a couple of minutes. I told him it would be my pleasure. (I was actually quite glad to get the opportunity to rest.) Ahead of us about another hundred yards was a little knoll, upon the very top of which was a huge, ancient oak tree. He suggested we sit down there. I said OK.

When we got to the knoll, we sat down with our backs leaning against the giant tree. From that spot you could see down across the pasture toward the buffalo's home corral and hay barn. Farther off in the distance was another valley; even farther off yet were more mountains. All I could think of as we first sat down was how beautiful the view was; it was like all of the world was stretched out in front of me. After giving ourselves a couple of minutes to take it all in, we resumed our conversation.

The thoughts I had regarding his low birth rates and the poor growth of his calves centered mainly around genetics and nutrition. I suggested the possibility that, due to the relatively small number of buffalo in the world, it was possible that the male that he was using for breeding might be too closely related to his cows. This would lead to an increase in birth defects. I also recommended that he supplement the herd with vitamins and minerals. I pointed out to him that even though his animals were well fed with pasture grass and hay, the soils in our area had been farmed for so long that most were deficient in some very critical trace elements and minerals. Without these important nutritional ingredients in their diets, it would be difficult to maintain good reproductive health and optimal growth.

As I spoke to this gentle old man, I witnessed, for the very first time in my veterinary career, the phenomenon that I would experience with nearly every client I would interact with for as long as I was to practice medicine: I realized at that moment that my clients, from now on, would be listening to and hanging upon every single word coming out of my mouth and that I might actually do some good in this world. I have to admit that at the time, this revelation made me a little bit scared and nervous.

And so it went. For about ten minutes, the old man asked me questions, and I answered them to the best of my ability. After we were finished, and just as I was getting a little restless to begin heading down toward the barns where the son would probably be waiting for us, the herd ambled over to a small man-made pond located about forty feet off to our right. There, now calm and content at being back home after their adventures, they drank at the water's edge. When they'd all drunk their fill, they started to walk away. All of them that is, except two baby calves.

As we sat there watching, the two little buffalo jumped into the shallow pond up to their knees and began to splash around and frolic in the muddy water. One would jump up, bring his head down through the water, and shower his herd mate. The other critter, in turn, would get excited, shake his head, dance up and down, bellow out a happy little buffalo noise, and then splash his buddy in return. It was quite a charming sight.

During this time, I happened to look over at the father and saw in his countenance the look of a man who was at peace with the world. And as I watched him watching these two glorious young creatures romping around like they hadn't a care in the universe, he must have sensed me looking at him, because he turned toward me. As he smiled one of the biggest smiles I'd ever seen, he pointed to his two playful buffalo calves and said, "Son, have you ever seen anything more beautiful that?"

I turned back toward the direction he was pointing and saw exactly what he meant. Farther beyond the buffalo, the afternoon sun hovered just above the infinite horizon in a brilliant, baby-blue sky. The midautumn foliage on the distant hills glowed as if on fire with red and orange and golden and crimson-colored leaves. And as I sat with that holy man on the top of that mountain under that magnificent old oak tree, I had to agree with what he said to me: It was indeed the most beautiful sight I'd ever seen in my life.

I turned toward the old man and saw that he was now looking at me. I was so overwhelmed, I couldn't speak. I felt like I'd been given a sacred look at the world as seen by the first man in the first garden; a revelation of the world before man's fall from grace; a vision of what the world could be if we all would just give it a chance. He nodded his head slightly as if he knew precisely what I had just witnessed.

We stayed for a couple of minutes more at that hallowed spot, and then we started back down the pasture toward the barns. Waiting there was the old man's son. And as I looked toward the highway, just outside the compound gate was a county sheriff's cruiser. After the old man and I climbed over the fence, the son said the deputy was waiting for me. Apparently, my partner had reported me missing, and a large manhunt had been organized to try to find me. Because it was getting late, I had to make my good-byes with the father and son a little briefer than I'd wanted to. The old man thanked me for my help, both in capturing the buffalo and for my advice with regards to their health care. We shook hands, and because the deputy wasn't allowed to enter onto the reservation property, I walked through the gate to the waiting police car, hopped in, and we drove away.

PostScript

As I was riding with the deputy back to his headquarters where Dr. Peter was waiting, he asked me how I'd ever managed to end up on the reservation. I then told him all that had happened to me that day. He was quite surprised to hear it because most non-Onondagas were rarely allowed to enter the reservation.

He then asked me if I knew who the elderly gentleman was who I'd spent the afternoon with. I told him I didn't. The deputy explained that the old man was Chief Leon Shenandoah, the leader not only of the Onondagas, but the head man of entire Iroquois Confederacy. "The Chief has traveled all over the world and has met presidents and kings!" he concluded, admiration in his voice.

I sat there stunned. I had just met this great man, and I hadn't even known it. Later on, as Dr. Peter and I were driving back to the vet college, more than once I laughed to myself as I recalled him standing there eating his bologna sandwich. I remembered thinking to myself as I rode with Chief Shenandoah and his son in their little Toyota pickup, that when he spoke on the CB radio, the people on the other end kept referring to him as "The Big Kahuna."

When I was back in class a few days later, I mentioned the whole adventure to a Native-American classmate of mine, Eaglefeather. He was especially interested in the vision like scene I described to him as Chief Shenandoah and I were sitting under the tree in the buffalos' pasture.

Eaglefeather then told me that the chief was the one who had given me this special insight, probably as a thank-you for my help, and that I should consider myself truly blessed.

And Eaglefeather was right. I was truly blessed.

CHAPTER TWO

EVERYTHING I NEEDED TO KNOW

Although it seems like about a thousand years ago, one of my earliest memories of vet school was a lecture given to my first-year classmates and me near the middle of our college's orientation week. The professor, a nice, young, and well-meaning fellow, gave a lecture about human behavior based loosely upon a popular book at the time titled *All I Really Need to Know I Learned in Kindergarten*. I can't remember precisely all of the little tidbits of wisdom he was trying to get across, but it had to do with something about holding hands, and smiling, and cleaning up after oneself.

I remember, as I sat there listening to the New Age wisdom he was preaching, that I couldn't help wondering what planet this guy might be from.

"Whoa!" I said to myself. "This guy's been in the ivory tower la la land just a little bit too long." I remember hoping that all of the professors at this great university weren't going to be like him. (They weren't.)

Perhaps my cynicism was the result of having been quite a bit older than him and the rest of my classmates, and that because of this advanced age, I'd had the experience of taking a considerable amount of hard knocks, all compliments of the real world. For example, nothing I learned in kindergarten could have ever prepared me for what I would need to know about how to survive four years in the U.S. Navy.

To the best of my recollection, I'd learned nothing from my kindergarten teacher about how to load five-inch Zuni rockets into a launching pod without setting off the explosive charges with the stray voltage in my body; she never warned me that one thing you absolutely never do in the Navy is refer to a salty old master chief petty officer as "hey dude"; nor was anything mentioned about handling all of the wonders and delights that existed for a bachelor teenager on a weekend R and R in the Philippine Islands or Hong Kong.

Likewise, later on in my life, when my wife and I operated our own dairy farm, not one word of my kindergarten instructor taught me anything about how to fix a frozen and busted iron water pipe on Christmas Eve, with all of the hardware stores in the world closed for the holiday, and all the while having to listen to a barn full of screaming, thirsty cows; nothing was said about how to cope with the ignorant new neighbors, who, knowing full well they were moving in next to a working dairy farm, nonetheless spent all of their spare time harassing us about how much our cows' manure smelled; and finally, to the best of my recollection, my kindergarten teacher did nothing to prepare us for dealing with unethical cattle dealers who had a million sly and sneaky tactics for selling us the occasional three-titted (instead of the normal four) milk cow.

However, I did go on to learn a lot of marvelous and wonderful things in my four long years of vet school. I guess if I had to put a number on them, they would probably total in the millions: how and why most diseases and illnesses happen, how to provide medical therapies and drugs to alleviate pain and suffering, and how to do astonishing surgeries to save lives. And I'm thankful to God for the opportunity to have had the benefit of those great humanitarians and gifted teachers. But just like kindergarten, not everything I needed to know about surviving in the world of private veterinary practice I learned in vet school.

It started the second day of my first and only (I would start my own practice the next year) job as a new veterinarian. I had been given the tasks of that afternoon's surgeries, which consisted of having to spay three cats and one dog. I jumped right in doing the first cat spay, cocky and confident, using all of the wonderful techniques I learned in school.

The senior partner stopped in to wish me luck. Remembering the words of many of my surgical lectures: "Great surgeons make great incisions," I proceeded to make a big cut in the cat's belly in order to get good exposure to the abdomen. Once inside, I confidently went through all of the complicated triple clamping techniques and double ligature suturing methods for tying off and removing the cat's ovaries and uterus.

I then spent the better part of a half hour sewing up the big hole I'd made in the poor cat's belly. Quite proud of myself for having finished the spay in just slightly over an hour, I then proceeded to do the same thing on the next cat. A couple of times during the surgery, the senior partner stopped by to watch. Seeing I was almost done with the second cat, he stuck around till I finished. I, in my new-graduate arrogance, thought he might be watching me to pick up on a new technique.

After finishing this second cat, and just before starting the third, the doctor finally spoke. I could detect a slight note of irritation in his voice. "Richard," he said, "you're driving me crazy watching you do all of that silly and unnecessary crap. Is that how they teach you to do surgery these days?"

A little bit surprised (and worried) by his tone of voice, I answered, "Yeah, Doc, it is."

Shaking his head and mumbling something to himself about those damned college boys, he smiled that big old Irish smile I would later discover he was so famous for and said to me, "Richard, they teach you a lot of wonderful things in vet school, and it's important to know all of the precise and exact methods of doing certain medical procedures.

When you're at a great institution like our vet school, you have all of the time and money in the world to get things done. But out here in the real world, there are a lot of little tricks you need to learn if you're ever going to survive in private practice and to be able to really help people. With your permission, let me show you the right way to do this surgery."

"Doc," I said, "I'd be honored."

He then scrubbed up and gloved, and proceeded to show me the most amazing things. In about fifteen minutes, he showed me how to do a spay surgery that was easier to do, with less stress on the patient, and accomplished in one-third of the time. I was in awe at the ease and simplicity of what I'd just been shown.

"I've been doing these cats and dogs this way for over forty years," he said as he removed his surgery gloves. "Never, Richard, has one ever gone bad." Grateful beyond words, I thanked him for his kindness and patient understanding; to this very day, I still use his techniques (as does just about every other successful private practitioner I've met).

During the remainder of the year, I worked under the guidance of Doc and the other associates, and they taught me many, many wonderful things, transforming me from a cocky wet-behind-the-ears college boy into a real veterinarian. But even with all of their help, there was one case, which when I think about it, still sends a shiver up my spine and baffles me to this very day.

It was a cold and rainy October Saturday night, and it was my weekend to be on call. All three of the associate doctors were out of town. I'd just been awakened out of a sound sleep by the answering service. "Doctor, there's a screaming owner with a seizuring dog that needs to talk to you." After giving me the phone number, the answering service lady added, "Good luck with this one, Doc, I think you're gonna need it!"

After collecting myself for a couple of seconds, I dialed the owner's number. Before I could even get in a hello, the terrified owner screamed out at the top of her lungs, "Duke is seizuring really bad. He won't snap out of it. What are we gonna do?" I could almost feel the wave of relief surging over the phone line as I told her to bring the dog right in.

As I got up and got dressed to head in to the hospital, I found myself a little bit excited; this was going to be my first real-life seizure. Oh, I'd seen a thousand seizures on film and video tape as a vet student, and I'd also helped care for and medicate animals already stabilized by doctors in the vet college's emergency room. But this would be my very first, genuine, seizuring patient.

The drive to the hospital gave me time to mentally review all of the proper procedures and treatment options. In my mind's eye, I saw myself calmly weighing the dog, drawing up the carefully calculated amount of drug into the hypodermic syringe, effortlessly finding a nice, big vein in the dog's foreleg, and then slowly injecting the drug into the patient, ultimately bringing about blessed relief for the beleaguered pet.

As I barreled into the driveway of the hospital, my first disenchantment of the evening took place. There, standing under the front door awning, was the screaming lady, her cranky-looking husband, and old Duke, who was the biggest Weimaraner I'd ever seen in my life, just standing there panting and wagging his little stump of a tail like he hadn't a problem in the whole world. Yes, dear reader, I'll admit that at that very moment, on that cold October evening, I was a bit perturbed at the sight of old Duke so healthy and happy.

Letting the clients into the exam room, I waited for just a second before asking (as calmly as I could), "What happened to the seizuring dog?"

The husband, sensing my frustration, meekly answered, "I don't know, Doc. After we hung up the phone, he just kinda snapped out of it."

Suppressing a growl, I then started going through the motions of taking a thorough history and doing a physical exam, when all of a sudden, chaos erupted. Old Duke, without the slightest warning, let out a wail, flopped to the floor onto his side, and started flapping his jaw and thrashing and paddling about with all four feet.

It never ceases to amaze me how different the real world is compared to textbook learning. Seeing this poor old dog flailing about on the exam room floor with thick, stringy saliva gushing from his mouth, with feces and urine spewing from the other end, and all the while, his owners wailing for me to do something, just absolutely scared the daylights out of me.

So I rushed into the hospital's treatment room, fumbled around finding the key to the controlled-drug box, and got out the drug needed to stop the seizure. Because I didn't have time to weigh the dog beforehand, any attempt at a textbook-accurate drug dose was now just a distant fantasy. I just drew up as close as possible the amount of drug I would need and ran back to the exam room.

By now the floor of the exam room was awash in a soup of saliva, urine, blood (Old Duke smashed his nose and forehead on the corner of the exam table), and mushed-up feces. As I stood there observing the carnage, I had my second disillusionment of the night.

I thought back to the vet school lectures on how to properly give an intravenous injection. The professor demonstrated for us how an assistant should hold off the animal's vein just above the elbow so it could readily be seen; cautioned us on how you should thoroughly swab the injection site with an alcohol pad in order to reduce the risk of infection; reminded us to make sure that, after injecting the needle into the vein, we gently draw back on the plunger, looking for blood to insure you indeed have the needle in the vein; and, finally, how you should put your thumb over the injection site for several seconds in order to avoid needless hemorrhaging.

The professor said not one word about what to do if you're out in the boonies, by yourself, in the middle of the night, with a big fat dog lying on its side in a pool of body fluids, with all four of his legs doing the polka in double time—all the while his owners shrieking in the background for you to "Please! Please! *DO SOMETHING!*"

After several unsuccessful tries, I finally managed to get a good vein. After injecting the syringe full of drug, I had my third disillusionment of the evening: nothing happened. The shot didn't work. By this time, I found myself thinking that maybe this veterinary medicine wasn't that great a career choice. Maybe I should be selling curly fries at the carnival or operating a concession stand in the Caribbean that rents beach chairs and umbrellas to semiclad tourists.

Finally, in desperation—and because I would need to anesthetize the dog anyway in order to suture up the laceration in his forehead—I went back into the drug lockbox and drew up an injection that would simply knock the dog out. I could think of nothing else to do. And, thank God, it worked.

The owners were happy the dog stopped seizuring and went home for the evening. Old Duke must have been happier under anesthesia, because he stopped spewing forth all of his foul body contents. And I was happy (with the exception of having to clean up the exam room) because without any idea of what to do, I'd managed to stop Old Duke's seizures, got rid of his screaming parents, and was again at peace with the world.

I sewed the hole in Old Duke's scalp, put him into a big cage, and went home to salvage what I could of a night's sleep.

When the answering service called a few hours later to tell me about a farmer having trouble with delivering a calf, I dragged myself out of bed, got dressed again, and headed out into the morning. But before driving out into the countryside, I decided to stop and check on my seizuring patient. Expecting the worst, I was surprised to find him bright and alert, standing up in his cage, and wanting desperately to go outside and pee.

Later that day, Old Duke went home as if nothing had ever happened. The owners declined to put him on any sort of seizure medication and, to the best of my knowledge, he never seizured again.

Several days later, I discussed the case during a rare morning coffee break with the doctor who'd taken the time weeks before to show me the practical tricks of the trade. I mentioned all of the possible reasons I could think of to cause seizuring in dogs— epilepsy, lead toxicity, head injuries, brain tumors, etc.—and then I asked him if he had any thoughts as to what might have cured this patient so quickly.

"You know, Richard, after you've been in this medical business for awhile, you're gonna see that most patients just don't read the book. Even as long as I've been at this stuff, sometimes all I can do with some of these patients is just stand back and scratch my head and wonder. In the case of your seizuring dog, maybe he just needed to bash his head against the corner of the exam room table and undergo a thorough purging in order to be cured. What do you think?"

I thought about what he just said, and I found myself amazingly comforted by his kind words. "It sounds good to me. Thanks, Doc."

Chapter Three

Guardian Angel

The scariest experience I ever had as a veterinarian took place on a beautiful springtime day in my second year of business. The memory of that day is so vivid in my mind that even now, as I write this story many years later, I can still feel the drafts of wind given off by the horse's hooves as they flailed just inches away from my nose; in my mind's eye, I still see the blinding flashes of sunlight as they reflected off the stainless steel fittings of the horse's halter; and I still feel the cold chill creep into my spine as I recall the freezing wetness of the spring snow on my skin as I lay helpless on my back. This was not the first time I'd almost been killed in my veterinary career, but it was certainly the worst. I vowed to myself after that day that I'd never put myself into that sort of situation again.

The whole ordeal started out with a simple phone call from the horse's owner. The man had called because he needed to have his four-year-old Arab stallion gelded (castrated). I recall that I'd had some concern about castrating a horse of that age, especially after the owner told me why he'd waited so long to do the operation. "Oh, I wanted to stud him out a few times because of his superior bloodline; I thought I might be able get a couple of colts from him. But I'll tell ya, Doc, lately he's been getting a little bit ornery, and now he's just about out of control." After a couple of seconds of silence, he added, "He's so bad now, Doc, that I can't even get him out of his stall without risking my life."

When he told me this, I almost backed out of doing the job. I'd done several castrations, both in vet school and in my practice, and although the surgery wasn't that big a deal (it's probably a big deal to the animal getting castrated), I just wasn't all that fond of doing them; it just gave me the creeps. But I was just starting out in business, and I needed the money, and so, without giving the job any more thought, I said I'd do it. I told the owner I'd be there in a couple of hours. After rounding up all of the equipment I'd need for the surgery, I loaded it up into my vetmobile.

As I was backing out of the driveway, I suddenly remembered that my friend and colleague, Dr. Al, had told me that if I ever needed help, to give him a call. He, too, was just starting out in business at the time, and better yet, he specialized in treating horses. I wavered back and forth as to whether or not to bother him, and I almost didn't.

But as I backed out onto the highway and shifted my old vetmobile into drive, an overwhelming thought entered my mind and shouted to me at the top of its lungs, "Richard! Get yourself back to your house and call Dr. Al and get him to help you!" And so, not wanting to argue with myself, I pulled back into my driveway, went inside my house, and called him up. The decision to bring him along to help me saved my life.

Over the years, I've learned to heed these mental warnings—especially when they're hollered at me. Some people call these subconscious flashes of insights *intuition*. Some refer to them as instinct. I—and I hope not to sound too crazy—regard these premonitions as gifts of Divine inspiration from my Guardian Angel.

I have a Guardian Angel, and for as long as I can remember, I've had this Guardian Angel. He (I know he is a he because, as I'll tell you in a few minutes, I've actually seen him) has watched over me, protected me from several near deaths, and has gently guided me to become everything I am today.

He was with me when, as a young teenager, I would walk down Roger's Hollow Road in the dead of night to the Saturday night square dances at the grange hall. He guided and protected me from my own ignorance during my four wild years in the U.S. Navy. While living alone on one of my parents' dairy farms, he sent me another angel, one who was looking for a summer job milking cows; she would turn out to be my future wife, Theresa.

When I decided in later life to become a veterinarian, he manifested himself in the forms of many, many, miraculous and gifted—and in my case, exceptionally patient—teachers; I know this to be so because there's no way that an old farm boy like me, who barely made it through high school twenty years earlier, could have ever done what I did without Heavenly intervention.

And he's with me still.

But before I continue with how he intervened in saving my life on that gorgeous springtime morning, I can almost hear readers of this story asking, "Come on, Doc, tell us the story of when you saw this Guardian Angel of yours."

Back in my Navy days, when tied up in port, I, and nearly all of my shipmates, would often go out after work and have a few beers.

One of the favorite spots my mates and I used to go to when we were in San Francisco was a big country Western bar down in San Jose, California, called Cow Town. It was about an hour's drive south of the city. One evening, after a particularly hard day of work, I decided to drive down by myself for just a few beers and to listen to the music. The beer tasted quite good that evening, so I ended up staying until closing. (And yes, I did cut myself off the beer and drank only ginger ale for the last couple of hours.)

After closing—and extremely tired—I started out on the long drive back to my ship. For those who may not know it, the freeway between San Jose and San Francisco, in places, is about six lanes wide and as straight as a rifle shot. I was clipping steadily along at about sixty miles per hour in my old cherry-red, 1965 Chevy Impala; I had the convertible top down. As I drove along, however, I felt myself being seriously overcome with a heavy, heavy urge to fall asleep. I knew I was in severe danger, but for reasons that I still don't understand, I couldn't stop myself. I just closed my eyes.

Almost as soon as I did, I heard a voice shout to me, "Richard!" Somewhat startled, I cracked my eyelids open just enough to glance off to the right-hand shoulder of the road. And there, standing sixty or seventy feet tall, was a man. His skin and clothing were the color of grayish white marble. When I glanced upward at his face, I could see he was looking me directly in the eye. I'm not lying when I tell you that this eyeball-to-eyeball thing between us got my direct attention. I snapped out of my stupor, and as I drove past this apparition, his head turned and his eyes literally followed me as I whizzed on by. I watched him until I could no longer twist my neck around far enough to see him. Needless to say, I was now wide awake.

Another time that I actually felt his presence was while still a student in vet school. It was on a late autumn Saturday afternoon. Theresa and I were in our garden digging up our crop of potatoes when, out of the blue, an old pickup truck stopped by the road near where we were working. A man got out, walked over to where we were working, and identified himself as a neighbor who lived about ten miles up the road. He had heard I was a vet and then said that he had a beef cow who was having trouble calving. I told him that I was still just a student but that I'd had a huge amount of experience in delivering baby calves on both my and my parents' farms, and I'd be willing to see what I could do. I could tell he was happy to hear this.

And so my wife and I got into our car and followed him up to his farm. He took us around back of his fallen-down barn and there, tied to an old piece of iron farm machinery, was a large black angus mama cow. She had evidently been trying to have her baby for quite some time because she was lying flat out on her side, exhausted.

I knelt down on the ground behind her and tried to figure out what was wrong. As I pushed my arm up inside of her birth canal, I discovered immediately that the calf had its left front foot hooked back around inside the mother. I remember thinking to myself that this would be a piece of cake. No problem, I'd successfully delivered calves with this difficulty a hundred times before.

I then proceeded to push the calf back up inside the mother's birth canal just a bit so I would have a little more room to work. This extra room allowed me to manipulate the twisted-around foot into the proper position for delivery. I then tied a couple of pieces of baling twine around the calf's feet, and, with the help of the farmer, pulled the baby out. When the calf was safely out and on the ground, we pulled him several feet off to the side in order to get him out of the puddle of birthing fluids. As I stayed with the calf to make sure he drained all of the mucus and fluids out of his airways, I told the farmer to go untie the mother so she could get up and come over to start licking the baby. This was a big mistake!

Before I had a chance to even think about it, the mother cow, who, just seconds before, had been lying there as quietly as can be, scrambled to her feet, let out a big groan, and turned toward me. The second she saw me kneeling there next to her baby, she let out a blood-curdling bellow and started charging at me. But because I was surrounded by old farm machinery on three sides of me, and the wet and slippery calf on another side, I was trapped; there was no way I could get out from in front of this mad, overly protective mother. The best I could do was lie down, scrunch up into a ball, and pray she didn't trample me too badly.

A split second later, as I lay there on the ground, I saw her out of the corner of my eye becoming airborne as she started leaping over the piece of iron machinery that separated us. Covering my head with my hands, I braced myself for the half ton of angry cow landing on my head and crushing my brains out.

But then, in a flash, the most amazing thing happened. About a microsecond before the expected impact, I felt a strong wind on the back of my exposed neck blowing hard across the ground from behind me. This was followed a split second later by the grinding of her two front feet as they slammed into the ground about a quarter of an inch away from my nose. *By golly,* I thought, *She missed me!*

As she lifted off, continuing her forward motion, the vacuum created by her feet as they left the ground dropped a load of dirt and debris into my face and eyes, momentarily blinding me. This turned out to be a blessing, because I was then saved from the dreadful sight of her hind feet as they pounded into the dirt even closer to my head than her front ones had.

When I finally came to my senses, the next thing I remember was the farmer yelling at me to get up and run. For the moment, at least, he was managing to hold back the cow with an old fence post. I scrambled to my feet and ran to the shelter of a nearby tractor.

A minute or so later, mama cow was over licking her baby and nuzzling the little darling like nothing had ever happened. I was still scared poopless, but it didn't matter a lick; I was alive. The strong breath of my Guardian Angel had been just enough to divert the giant beast from landing on her intended target, my thick old head. And I was grateful.

There would be many other times he would help me, and my hope is, that as I write this humble little story, I continue to find favor in his eyes as he carries out his Divine mission on behalf of our Lord. And, to make a long story even longer, I'll finish the original story I began with earlier.

After pulling back into my driveway, I went inside my house and called my friend, Dr. Al. He said he'd be happy to help me, and so we met about a half hour later at a coffee shop not far from the horse owner. After a quick cup of coffee and catching up on all of the gossip, we drove up to the horse farm in my vetmobile. The farmer met us in the dooryard, and then we all walked out to the barn together. He pointed out the stallion we were going to geld, and sure enough, he was a rotten little brat; he snorted and kicked at the stall door continuously with his front feet, and he just paced back and forth like a maniac. I asked the farmer how in the heck we were ever going to get him out of his stall. "Oh," he said, "he lets me take him out of the stall for cleaning, but that's it. I can't do anything else with him."

Dr. Al and I surveyed the situation and came to the conclusion that if the farmer could get the horse out of the stall, with a little extra effort, we (Dr. Al and I) might just be able to coax it outside to the front of the barn where we would be able to inject the anesthetic agent into the vein of his neck. After about an hour of ranting and raving, kicking and snorting, we managed to get the horse outside to the driveway. I was working the lead that was wrapped double around the horse's nose as Dr. Al stood by, ready to hand me the syringes of anesthesia when the time was right.

When it seemed like he was ready to calm down, Dr. Al handed me one of the syringes and I stuck it—like I was supposed to—into the jugular vein of the horse's neck. At the exact moment I did, the horse reared up on his hind legs, mad as a snake, and started thrashing at me with his front feet. I, who wasn't going to take any crap from any spoiled rotten horse, yanked down hard on his lead, hollering all the while for him to get down.

But this guy was as stubborn as I was. He just insisted on walking along on his hind feet, trying all the while to strike me with his front hooves. I didn't realize it at the time, but he was also backing me into a big pile of snow that had accumulated over the winter from the farmer plowing his driveway. And before I knew what had happened, I'd stepped a couple of feet into the melting, slushy snow, and my left boot got stuck. As it did so, I fell down, and my backward momentum twisted me around like a pretzel. I ended up with my chest upward and exposed to the flailing feet of that crazy horse. The son of a gun was hell-bent on trampling me to death.

And then a miracle happened. Dr. Al, who had played professional football in Italy in order to pay his way through vet school, saw what was happening, and without the slightest regard for his own safety, ran over and threw himself against the horse's left shoulder. He hit the horse so hard that it spun him completely around on his hind legs, so that before he even knew what happened, he ended up heading in the opposite direction. I was safe. My Guardian Angel, through Dr. Al, had saved my life.

But there's more to this story. Over the years I discovered another of the attributes of my Guardian Angel: He seems to have a sense of humor.

Sometimes, in order to get his point across, He adds additional effects. In this case, the horse, realizing he was now free, took off running. However, before he did, the horse had to take one last kick. The little brat's foot connected with his owner, who had been innocently standing by, watching the whole drama as it unfolded, and the blow broke both bones in the farmer's forearm.

The next day, a couple of the owner's relatives and I managed to get the horse cornered in a pasture, and then a couple of days later, they managed to get him back into the barn. The owner took all that happened as a sign to get rid of the horse. I, likewise, took it as a warning to stay as far away as I could from the beasts. I've heeded my Angel's warning and have never touched a horse since.

CHAPTER FOUR

BECAUSE GOD SAYS SO

One of the many great and time-honored traditions at the vet college where I went to school is that of Show-and-Tell. Although definitely not for the weak of stomach (and, indeed, not all of my colleagues attended the sessions), it was at Show-and-Tell where a lot of us soon-to-be doctors got our first serious look at what many animal diseases looks like, what they can feel like, and what they smell like.

The institution of Show-and-Tell exists in various forms and under different names at every medical and veterinary school in the world. It is a formal method of instructing medical students and professionals that has been around since the days of ancient Greece, when old Hippocrates himself, the father of medicine, would personally preside over the sessions.

Every Friday afternoon, all of us highly motivated students, interns, residents, and staff would all assemble for Show-and-Tell in the college's autopsy room. There in this small, crowded room, which perpetually smelled of a combination of rubbing alcohol, formaldehyde, chemical disinfectant, and bowel contents, we'd all sit on bleachers that had been set up around a large central stainless-steel table. On this table would be preserved specimens of diseased body tissues and organs that had been surgically removed from patients in the hospital as well as the remains of animals that had been sent in—or generously donated—to the school's pathology department by their owners or field veterinarians.

Here, in this amphitheater-like setting, under the guidance of a senior pathology professor, we would all respectfully look at, touch, and sometimes even smell the specimens of diseased body tissue so we would know what it was if we ever saw it again. After this, we would discuss in great detail everything known about that particular disease.

One of the great masters of this tradition is one of my former professors—and still a dear friend—Dr. John King. Although a giant in the field of pathology throughout the world, he especially takes very seriously his role of moderator during these Show-and-Tell sessions.

His favorite teaching technique during these sessions often goes as follows: While holding the remains of an animal or a sample of diseased tissue, he'd walk up to a student or an intern who was bold enough to sit in the front row of bleachers and ask her/him to explain why the animal he was holding died.

The student would look at the body or body organ, perhaps reach out to feel or smell the lesion, and then propose an explanation. If this person was correct, Dr. King would offer up lavish praise and congratulate the student on his/her exceptional brilliance. If the person didn't know the answer, he would say nothing, just sort of nod his head, and then move on to the next person. (Every once in a while, if he felt the student *should* have known the answer, he'd let out an exasperated, "ah-huh.") One thing you never did at Dr. King's Show-and-Tell sessions was to make a wild guess at the animal's cause of death. To do so was to incur his wrath. (I, of course, had to discover this fact the hard way.)

After everyone had a chance to view the specimen, he'd return to the center table and then proceed to discuss the animal's cause of death at length. When he was finished, he'd answer questions from the group and then move on to the next sample.

Every once in a while—maybe once every three or four sessions—Dr. King would circulate around with a tissue specimen and seem to be a little more solemn and serious in the task than he normally was. I recall that during one of these times, he stood before me holding the remains of a cat. He looked at me and said, "Dr. Orzeck, why did this cat die?"

(Even though many of us were still students, he used the title "Doctor" as a courtesy.)

I carefully looked at the animal's exposed body organs and chest cavity. I felt its heart, lungs, lymph nodes, everything, and had absolutely no idea of why the poor critter died. But not wanting to look like a complete idiot (I also might have even been trying to show off), I gave what I thought (at the time) was a pretty good answer. I should have known better.

Dr. King looked at me with that glare for which he was so famous and in no uncertain terms said, "Don't BS me, Orzeck!" [BS was not the exact phrase he used] and then he moved on to the next hapless student. It would turn out with this particular cat that no one seemed to have any idea of its cause of death.

After everyone had their chance to view the specimen, he again returned to the center table. He laid the cat's remains down onto the table and without saying another word, he started to pick up the next case. But before he could begin, one of my more courageous colleagues hollered out from the top row of bleachers, "So, Dr. King, why did this poor cat die?"

The room became so quiet that you could hear the Cornell bells chiming in the bell tower two miles down campus. Then Dr. King, one by one, looked us all squarely in the eyes, solemnly pointed his right hand to the ceiling, and, with the reverence of a saint, he said, "Because God said so."

That was all that was needed to be said about the matter.

In my day-to-day practice of veterinary medicine, I get this same question all the time: "So, Doc, please tell us why our cat/dog/parakeet/cow/horse died?" And I wish I had a quarter for all of the times that question has been asked since those days years ago in the postmortem room at vet school.

I believe that one of the truest absolutes that exists in us human beings is this driving, unquenchable, almost instinctive need to know why something happens: Why are we here? Why is there evil, struggle, and despair in our world? Why do bad things happen to good people? The greatest philosophers, theologians, and poets our world has ever produced have pondered these mysteries since the dawn of mankind, and we still don't have the exact answer. If you let it, the whole thing could drive you crazy.

But before I continue, I want to make it perfectly clear that in no way does this question ever annoy me. I believe with all my heart that if a client has a question, its my responsibility to answer. I understand the urge to know why and the overwhelming need to have closure. I'll be the first to admit that I also am guilty of the same behavior. I hope this story from my personal experience demonstrates this.

A few years ago, I got the notion to increase the value of my disability insurance. I had nearly gotten killed trying to castrate a four-year-old Arab stallion a few days before, and I wanted to make sure that, just in case I was ever seriously injured, we'd have enough to pay the mortgage on my clinic and my huge school loan.

Because I was a little older, the insurance company insisted on sending a nurse out to my home to give me a simple physical. And so I got my blood pressure checked, my weight measured, peed into a little cup, and gave about four tubes of blood. A couple of weeks later, I got a letter from the insurance company telling me I'd been turned down for the increase; the only reason they gave me was that I had protein in my urine.

I knew that if I was a dog, protein in my urine could be a sign of serious renal (kidney) disease. I followed the recommendations of the tiny print at the bottom of the rejection letter and set up an appointment with a doctor friend and client of mine who had a specialty in internal medicine. He, too, gave me a very thorough physical examination and sent me to a laboratory where I again peed into a cup and again gave the nurse four more tubes of blood.

A couple of days later, he gave me a call to tell me that, with the exception of my cholesterol being slightly elevated, all was normal. When I asked if there was protein in the urine, he said it was still there.

He then prescribed more tests specifically to evaluate my kidneys' actual ability to function. This time, however, instead of a tiny cup, I was given what looked like a giant moonshine jug to urinate into for the next twenty-four hours. I also had to give more blood (only one tube this time). And just like the first time, all of the tests came back normal. There still was just a little protein in the urine.

When we spoke on the phone, I asked him, "Doc, what does that mean?"

He answered that with everything else being normal, it probably meant nothing, and we just don't know for sure why it happens. I thanked him for everything he'd done and that was that. Although I haven't worried about it since the insurance company so coldly and tactlessly scared the poop out of me with their blunt form letter, in moments of quiet reflection, I wonder to this very day why I'm passing protein.

On my exam table lay an eighteen-year-old female Siamese named Ming, who was in the final stages of renal failure. A few days before, her owner brought her into my office with the chief complaint of the cat drinking a lot of water, urinating large volumes in her litter box, and rapid weight loss. During the physical examination, one of the first things I noticed was that despite drinking a huge amount of water, she was clinically dehydrated; her skin was as stiff as cardboard. When I looked into her mouth, her teeth were rotten and covered with a layer of tartar, and her breath was very foul; this was a sign of uremia. Her weight loss was of a special kind referred to medically as muscle wasting; she had not one shred of muscle on her bones.

As I palpated around Ming's abdomen and guts, I could feel that her kidneys were about half the size they should have been and were gnarly and lumpy feeling; they should normally feel about the size of a plum and just as smooth.

My suspicion was that Ming's kidneys were failing, and she didn't have long to live. I drew blood and sent it to the laboratory and tested her urine as well because the owner wanted to make sure. When the results came in, I called Ming's daddy, and I gently told him that the blood work and urine analysis confirmed my original diagnosis. He asked if he could bring Ming in to put her to sleep; she had deteriorated so quickly in the last two days that she could no longer get up. I told him it would be OK.

And sure enough, when he brought her in and set her on my exam table, sweet old Ming was nearly in a coma. She just lay there flat out. After I was finished and was wrapping her up in her favorite blanket, her owner asked me the question that has no answer. It is the same question I'm asked by 999 clients out of 1,000 who are faced with a disease in their animals: "Doc, why did this happen? What caused it?" Most of the times I can usually give a pretty good answer: old age, bad scarring from an old injury, cancer, etc. But once in a while, I have to tell the pet's mommy or daddy that I just don't know.

Clients rarely let me get away with this "I don't know" answer. And that's OK. I understand. Sometimes, if I think I can get away with it, I'll get a little bit more sophisticated and babble something like, "Medical researchers have not yet discovered the precise mechanism for this particular disease complex," or "The scientists who have been working on this affliction say they're expecting a break-through any time now; unfortunately, as of this moment, the true cause still eludes them."

Clients rarely let me off the hook with these answers either. And so most of the time I end up having a session of simple questions and answers. Regardless how full my waiting room is, I let the hearings take their course because in just about every case, this method works the best to satisfy the owner's sense of loss.

"Doc, do you think it's our well/municipal/spring water?"

I tell him it's not probable because if the water wasn't killing him, then it wouldn't kill his cat.

"Do you think it was a poisoning?"

I tell him it's possible, but not likely in an eighteen-year-old cat.

"Doc, could it have been from eating a mole, a house plant, a chocolate Hershey's Kiss, spaghetti sauce, dog food, cheese doodles?

I assure him that none of these things would likely have caused such a severe disease as Ming had.

But even after all this effort, some owners just won't let it go. And I can hear the exasperation obvious in their voice when they ask, "Doc, why did *my* cat die?"

At this point, I usually just stop talking for a couple of seconds to allow the client's frustration and tension to sort of dissipate. I then look him in the eye and turn his questions back at him.

"Sir, I just don't know why your cat developed kidney disease and died. You'd get just as good an answer from me by asking me why the sun rises. Why does one ten-year-old little girl develop a brain tumor and another doesn't? Why does a young and healthy mother get struck down in the prime of her life with multiple sclerosis or breast cancer?" And then I don't say a word.

After some time for quiet reflection, the answer I get is, "Doctor, I don't know."

Another dear client brings in her big, highly spirited, male golden retriever named Jack. At six years of age he has begun seizuring a couple of times a month. Jack's mommy, a medical doctor herself in a speciality practice, would like to know the reason why.

I explain that seizures in dogs can occur for many reasons. Sometimes there is an underlying problem with the liver or kidneys that brings on the attacks. Once in a while it can be the result of a severe blow to the head. Rarely, and almost exclusively in old age, a brain tumor can be the cause. But I emphasized to her that these causes turn out to be the rare exception. Almost always, the biggest reason for seizuring in dogs is just plain epilepsy. And epilepsy, as a disease, is not well understood; its cause is—you guessed it—not known.

And so I took a careful history of Jack's life, concentrating on possible traumas and accidents he may have had. His physical examination was normal.

When his blood work returned from the laboratory, it showed that all was normal with his liver and kidneys. This sort of left us with the diagnosis of idiopathic epilepsy.

I was a little indecisive as to whether or not I should just let my diagnosis of epilepsy stand on its own or whether I should give Jack's owner my interpretation of what the term means. (After all, we'd both been to medical school and therefore knew at great length the ins and outs of the brain's anatomy, physiology, and function.) But I could tell by her worried expression that maybe I'd better give her my thoughts and interpretation of Jack's disease. From my own personal experience, I know its hard to concentrate and think objectively when the patient in question is your own animal. I gave it my best shot.

I reminded her that epilepsy is a disease in which a part of the brain begins to discharge electrical current uncontrollably. This uncontrolled discharge then shows up in the animal's body as the twitching and muscle spasms we observe during a seizure. When medical people add the term *idiopathic* to the disease of epilepsy, its just a fancy way of saying that we just don't know why or how it happens.

As I was explaining all this to Jack's mommy, I could tell that she was having trouble with my answers. Although she never actually said it, the old question was lurking in the background of her thoughts: *So, Doc, why is it happening to my dog?* Again, because she had a medical background, I further went on to explain how, over the years, my neurology professor had taken countless brains of animals whose owners had put them to sleep because of seizuring. He sectioned these brain tissues into thin slices. He then examined under a microscope every square millimeter of them, looking for a cause of the animal's epileptic seizures. He could not find a single answer as to why.

I let this last explanation kind of settle in a little bit before I continued. As I watched Jake's mommy standing across the exam table from me, I could almost imagine her—as all us doctors do—going back to her medical school freshman anatomy class and visualizing the studies she had done on the human nervous system and the brain. I imagined her recalling the thousands of X rays, brain CT scans, and MRIs we've all had to look at one time or another. After a couple more seconds of silence, I stated the obvious.

"Doctor," I continued, "think about the patients or even friends or relatives you may have known over the years who've had trouble with seizures. In spite of all of the billions and billions of dollars spent on research, sophisticated diagnostic machines, and hospitals no one has yet been able to come up with an absolute cause of epilepsy. Asking why these seizures are happening to Jack would be like asking (and the reader of this story has heard this before), why does the sun rise? Why does one ten-year-old little girl develops a brain tumor and another doesn't? Why does a young and healthy mother get struck down in the prime of her life with multiple sclerosis or breast cancer?"

And so it goes. Sometimes we just have to accept the fact that there are no answers. I don't have a good reason why one puppy out of a litter of eleven should die of parvovirus and not the others. I wish I had a good answer for why a cat, who's crossed the same road a thousand times should, just one time, forget to look both ways and get hit by a car. I don't know why a young dog (or an innocent child, for that matter) should all of a sudden come down with cancer. The same question could be asked about plane crashes, deranged people killing the innocent, war and famine, and all other horrors. Sometimes the only answer that I can give is the one that old Dr. King taught me long ago when I was still a wet-behind-the-ears vet student: "Because God says so!"

CHAPTER FIVE

FIDO

At the time of this writing, my wife and I have six cats: Orville, the old man of the bunch; Elvis, a petite tortoiseshell female; Lezzard, an orange and white tiger kitty; Pole Kitty, another tortoiseshell who, unlike little Elvis, is quite rotund; The Blackest Kitty; and The Gray Cat.

Orville was given to my wife years ago by one of her coworkers. I brought home little Elvis as an eight-week-old kitten. She was one of about a hundred or so little kittens scampering and frolicking around at a dairy farm I'd visited earlier that day. I chose her out of the group to replace our other tortoiseshell cat, Pole Kitty, who had been missing for about a month. (Pole Kitty, of course, returned from her walkabout the same evening I brought Elvis home.)

Lezzard, whose name somehow evolved from its original Lucy, is the young one of the bunch. She was one of a brother-and-sister pair that a client brought into my office as seven-week-old kittens; the lady had found them in the hay mow of her horse barn and was getting them vaccinated in order to adopt them out. My wife had been looking for a couple of years for another orange shorthaired kitten to replace a dear cat of hers that I'd accidentally backed up over with the old family Buick a few years before, and so we adopted her. Pole Kitty, The Black Cat, and The Gray Cat, are all the result of my bringing home a teeny, tiny, gray and black tiger kitten named Fido. And Fido, bless her little heart, almost ended my veterinary career before it ever got started.

I had Fido literally thrust upon me in the spring of my freshman year at vet school. It was a Saturday morning, and I'd gotten up early in order to drive two hours back to my family's hometown in order to get a good deal on a pair of tires for my old pickup truck. (As its been since the dawn of higher education and probably will be forever, for those students like me who put themselves through college, it was—and still is—important to save every dime possible.)

Old man Potter's Tire Service was one of those old, rural, garage-type places that aren't all that common anymore. He and his nephew did everything they could to provide monumental cutomer service and keep costs of their tires down. Instead of a sterile waiting room with a squeaky-clean counter, plush chairs, and a magazine rack full of *Home and Gar-*

den magazines, this place had a desk in the corner piled high with tire and auto parts catalogs, stacks of tires from the floor to the ceiling, and two wooden kitchen chairs that could, without any great effort, be moved outside when the weather was nice. If you wanted to read anything other than a few copies of outdated *Hot Rod* magazines, you had to bring it along with you.

And that's what I'd done; I'd brought along my Infectious Diseases class notes to study as my tires were being changed. I found a small stack of tires off in one of the corners next to the front window and was sitting there as comfortable as can be, when out of nowhere, a wrecker truck pulled up out front. Hooked up to the back of the truck was an old, tan Chevy Malibu with both of the front doors missing. The driver of the tow truck, who I did not know, came walking into the waiting area where I was sitting, reached into the left front pocket of his greasy coveralls, and handed me a tiny ball of warm fur.

"Lyle tells me you're a vet," he said with a look of serious concern. "I found this here kitten under the front seat of that there car." He pointed out the window toward the Malibu. "Could you look at this kitten? I don't think it's doin' too good." He then turned and started walking away.

As I struggled with all my strength to get out of my improvised chair, all the while holding my precious class notes in one hand and a fragile little kitten in the other, I hollered out after him, "Wait a damn minute, I'm not a vet yet, I'm just a student. Hey, I don't want another cat!" But before I could get to my feet to stop him, he climbed back into the tow truck, ground it into first gear, and in a New York minute, he and the old Malibu were gone. "Poop, poop, poop!" I shouted out loud as I stormed into the garage's service bay to confront Lyle. [I must admit at this time that I didn't really use the word *poop*; I actually used the word's more explicit cousin.] "Lyle, your man just handed me this kitten and drove off."

Lyle, who was squatted down next to the right front wheel of my pickup, looked up at me, innocently smiling, and said, "Yeah, Hank's sorta like that." And then he turned and went back to tightening down the lug nuts on my tire.

"But Lyle, what am I gonna do with this kitten?"

Glancing up briefly from his work, he gave me one of those gentle but persuasive looks that let me know in no uncertain terms that he didn't want to be distracted by this minor point any longer. "Richard, please, just take the little guy home to Theresa, and she'll take good care of it. I know if anybody can save it, she can." (He knew Theresa almost as well as I did because they went to grade school together.)

After a few more seconds' pause, with me looking at him, and him looking at me, I finally backed down some and accepted my fate. "OK, Lyle, I'll see what we can do." I walked outside into the good light and gave the little kitten an exam.

The little thing was tiny; it couldn't have been more than four weeks old. Its eyes were crusted shut with what was probably a mild case of distemper, as was the poor thing's left nostril. But as bad as it looked, the little guy was still breathing well and had an OK amount of body weight. Realizing there was nothing I could do until I got home, I slipped the kitten into the left pocket of my flannel work shirt where it seemed to be quite content to stay. I, however, was still just a little disturbed at having this unwanted burden thrust upon me and so, in order to pacify myself, I decided to walk to an ice cream stand about a quarter of a mile down the block.

I hollered into the garage, "Lyle I'm walking over to the Dairy Queen for an ice cream cone. You want me to bring you something back?"

"No, thanks, Richard," he replied, "I got my lunch to eat yet."

So I walked down the street and into the store and bought myself a large vanilla soft ice cream cone. Since it was such a beautiful day, I decided to sit down at one of the picnic tables outside and lei-surely eat my cone. But after sitting there a couple of minutes, I began to feel a stirring in my shirt pocket. I looked down, and to my amazement, the little kitten had squirmed its way up to the top of the pocket and popped its tiny head out. With its front paws grasping the upper edge of the pocket and its little uncrusted nostril held high, it seemed to be scanning the air like a little radar beam as if it was trying to smell something. It was really strange.

Even though I knew it couldn't see anything through its crusty eyes, the little critter would fol-low the cone's every move. I'd bring it up to my mouth for a bite, and it would twist its head slowly upward; I'd lower the cone back down to the table-top, and it would turn its head down. It took me a couple of minutes before it dawned on me that the poor thing might be hungry and that the smell of the ice cream had roused it from its sleep.

And so, not quite sure what else to do, I brought the cone up toward the little kitten's mouth. After a couple of seconds of hesitation, it cautiously stuck its little tongue out and licked the ice cream. After a second of trying to decide whether it was good or bad, it again slowly stuck its tongue out and took another dainty lick. This was all it took. The next lick was a full frontal attack. It slammed its face into the ice cream and began gobbling it up like it hadn't eaten in years.

"Take it easy, big guy," I said as I pulled the cone away and ate a few bites of it myself, "there's plenty more." After about a minute, I put the cone back down in front of the kitten, and it again gulped little mouthful after little mouthful of the ice cream. And so we sat there on that beautiful, sunny springtime day, the two of us, eating an ice cream cone. When it was all done, the little kitten slid back down in my pocket and fell asleep.

I walked back to the garage, paid Lyle for the tires, thanked him for the excellent service (nothing was said at all about the kitten), got into my pickup, and began my long drive back home. Because I was a little afraid of the kitten peeing or pooping in my pocket, I made a little bed out of an old T-shirt that had been left in the truck and set the cat down in it. Since my journey home would take me past the vet school, I decided to stop and see if I could get one of the professors or senior students to perhaps examine the kitten and give me some medicine.

Leaving the kitten in the truck, I walked in the back door and, with no effort at all, found a forthyear student who was thrilled to help me. And so I walked back out to the parking lot and got the kitten. In order to save time in walking all the way around to the back door of the clinic again, I made the disastrous mistake of going in through the front desk reception area.

Here, seeing the kitten in my hands, the ever vigilant receptionists, not knowing who I was (again, I was still in my first-year and hadn't as yet become acquainted with these ladies) insisted on not letting me into the hospital. I told them very politely that I was a first-year student, that I had this dying kitten I just found, and that a senior student was waiting for me out on the wards in order to help it out.

My being at their desk wanting to enter the hospital with a sick kitten was an event they weren't prepared to handle, and so the ladies all decided to have a conference in order to figure out what to do. And for some reason, which to this very day I still don't understand, they told me I couldn't come in. When I asked them why, they said it was the policy.

When I look back at that moment, I realize they were just doing what they were supposed to do. What I should have done was smile and politely thank them for their feeble efforts. Then, I should have walked out the front door, walked around the hospital building, and just come in the back way. But I didn't.

Maybe I was just fed up at being taken advantage of that day; first by the tow truck driver, then the mechanic, and now by these indifferent and seemingly mindless receptionists. As I stood there at that desk staring at the self-satisfied look on their faces, an impatient and somewhat arrogant attitude started to come over me. *Richard*, I said to myself, *the heck with these ladies. Who are they to tell you that you can't come into this hospital? You're a student here, and the professors told you on the very first day of classes that as a student, you could go anywhere in the hospital you wanted to at any time.*

And so, not paying one bit of attention to their rantings and ravings, without saying another word, I just walked past their desk and through the door of the hospital. I smiled to myself at my cockiness.

I quickly found the senior student, handed her the tiny kitten, and she anxiously began examining it. She informed me that, with the exception of the eyes and upper respiratory tract, the little creature wasn't in all that bad a shape. The most likely cause of its problems was probably a mild form of distemper. She told me I'd be learning about the disease pretty soon in my Infectious Diseases class. I also learned at this time that the kitten was a little girl.

After she finished the examination, we all walked together to the clinic's treatment room. Here she got some saline-soaked gauze pads and gently began to moisten the crusts on the kitty's eyes. As we stood there waiting for the crusts to soften, I heard a woman's voice behind me in the hallway say, "There he is, Doctor; that's him. He doesn't belong in here!" And as I turned around to see what would happen next, there in front of me was the biggest darn hippy looking guy I'd ever seen. I had no idea who he was.

Oh boy, Rich, I said to myself, *what are you gonna do now?* And about the same time I thought this, a dark notion crossed my mind: *This silly little kitten is gonna get me thrown out of vet school!*

As we stood there looking at each other, trying to figure out what to do next, he paused for a moment, turned to the lady still anxiously waiting in the hall, and said with calm authority, "It's OK, I'll take care of it from here."

I could tell by her disappointed groan she wasn't too happy about having to leave and so she just stood there. I'm sure she was hoping to see me flogged to within an inch of my life. And seeing she wasn't about to leave without a fight, the doctor, this time with authority, once again said, "Ma'am, I told you I'd take care of this. Now please return to your desk." This time she listened.

He then turned back around, and I could tell by the look on his face that he was obviously quite perturbed with the whole situation. He looked at me, and I looked at him, and after a couple of seconds, he snarled, "My name is Dr. Haight-Ashbury [not his real name]. I'm in charge of the clinics. Are you a student here?"

I stood there, holding the tiny kitten up in my in hand, without the slightest idea of what to do next. The senior student, like nothing was wrong at all, was still patiently and lovingly trying to soak its little eyes open. A billion thoughts were going through my mind. This guy looked pretty angry. My instinct was to fight, to take the offensive, but a little voice told me to be patient and just take it easy. From the experience of my first four years of college, I knew that many professors have quite a fragile ego. I also knew that they had nearly absolute power and could, if they put their minds to it, get me thrown out.

And so, looking him squarely in the eye, in my most humble tone of voice, I answered, "Yes, sir, I'm a first-year student. My name is Richard, and I'm truly sorry to have caused all of this trouble."

A couple more seconds passed, and there we were, still eye to eye. The senior student, like she hadn't a worry in the world, was still working on the little kitten's eyes. In the course of all this, she'd managed to successfully get one eye pried open. Finally, the professor broke the silence. "Richard," he said, "next time, do us all a big favor and come in the back way." As his stern expression faded away and a smile filled his face, he added, "Those ladies up front can be a real pain in the neck, but they're just doing their job."

Relieved beyond words, I gratefully said, "Thank you, sir, I will." And before I could say any more, he turned and walked over to where the senior-year student was working on the kitten and the two of them began a discussion about possible therapies for treating the animal. The whole situation turned into a great learning experience for both of us.

When we all were done, and as he turned to leave, we shook hands. "Richard, welcome to the family."

After he was gone, the senior student and I finished working on the kitten. She and the professor had come to the conclusion that it had a slight upper-respiratory infection as a result of a mild form of distemper. The eye and nostril crusts were probably the result of a secondary bacterial infection. The kitten would do just fine after a week of antibiotic therapy.

As the student was mixing up the powdered antibiotics and preparing the prescription label, I commented to her on how cool and calm she had remained during the whole episode with the professor.

She just laughed.

I said, "Weren't you worried about catching hell from him and getting in trouble?"

"Absolutely not, and you'll see this as you go along. The college wants us to learn this stuff any way we can. That's why they tell us we can come in to the hospital any time we want. And besides, that was Dr. Haight-Ashbury; you'll have his dermatology class next fall. You'll see for yourself he's a wonderful teacher and a super-good guy."

And indeed, in the fall, I took his class, and he was a masterful teacher. We would interact about a thousand more times in the remaining three years of vet school both in the classroom and in the clinic, and we remain good friends to this day.

I then took the kitten home and, just as Lyle said, Theresa nursed her back to health. For no particular reason, we named her Fido. And, before we could afford to have Fido spayed, she blessed us with Pole Kitty and The Gray Cat. And before we could afford to get her fixed, The Gray Cat blessed us with The Black Cat.

CHAPTER SIX

SAINTS AMONG US

"Hello, Doctor, this is Emma again."

"How you doing, Emma?" I asked, even though the subdued and slightly frustrated tone in her voice on the other end of the phone line had already answered the question for me.

"I guess I'm OK. The only trouble, Doctor, is that I just caught me another one. Is there any way you could somehow slip her in for surgery today?"

"No problem, Emma," I said, "Just bring the cat in and leave it with Theresa. I'll get to her as soon as I can later this afternoon."

My dear old friend and client, Emma, is typical of her kind. She's an adorable, plain-spoken, tiny, elderly widow on a small pension and Social Security who suffers from a fairly common problem:

somehow or another, an endless torrent of cats—most of them pregnant or with kittens—just keep showing up in her yard and on her back porch. And so she, at great financial hardship, has decided to take it upon herself to try her best to take care of each and every one of the little critters.

At least once every two weeks, she comes to my clinic carrying a borrowed Havahart live trap that's almost as long as she is tall. In the cage would be a wild-eyed, hissing and snarling, pissed off, feral cat that she'd carefully—and with the most infinite patience—managed to catch in order that the little darling could get its shots and be spayed or neutered. I never ceased to be amazed at her skill in catching these wild beasts.

"Emma," I'd ask as we were filling out the surgery form, "I need to have a name for the rabies registration form. What do you want to call this one?"

After a couple of seconds to ponder the question, she'd say, "Have we used the name Blackie in a while?"

"Yes we did, Emma, the last two times."

"Oh darn," she'd say, obviously frustrated by this seemingly dauntless task. After another couple of seconds of thoughtful consideration, she'd say, "Doctor, I guess if its a boy you can name him Tom. If its a girl, just name her Baby."

"No problem, Emma. Tom or Baby it will be."

To this very day, in the small, rural village where Emma lived, there probably are still about a dozen

Toms or Babies—as well as about twenty-five Blackies, Tigers, Snowballs, and Callies—all still alive and happy and healthy because of the infinite love and concern of this one sweet and caring lady.

I'm not quite sure why anyone would ever want to do so, but if someday I was ever asked to make a list of what I thought were absolute and universal human traits, right up there near the very top of the list (just after a mother's love and man's need to search for a meaning to his earthly life), I would have to place the worldwide phenomenon of the existence of cat ladies.

Cat ladies. We've all heard of them. They are the kind souls who seem to have dedicated their lives to the safety and welfare of cats everywhere. Everybody knows at least one of them. Many people probably know several. I'll even go so far as to say that some of you out there reading this story right now may actually be one yourselves.

It's my opinion that every city, village, or town on our planet has at least one cat lady. In my travels of this world, I've seen these compassionate souls and their beloved cats every place I've gone: from a lonely (very lonely) gas station on the highway between Jericho and the Sea of Galilee in Israel's Jordan River valley, to a carpet seller's stall located within the shadow of the magnificent Blue Mosque in the ancient city of Istanbul; from a souvenir shop in the French village of Caen near the hallowed beaches of Normandy, to a mountaintop Hindu temple on the enchanted Pacific island of Bali.

Likewise, I've seen evidence strongly suggesting the existence of cat ladies (by the large numbers of cats sunning themselves) in the windows of a New York City Park Avenue town house, on the roof of a mansion along Chicago's Lake Michigan, as well as on the third-story balcony of an apartment building in San Francisco's North Beach.

Closer to home, I have two wonderful neighbors who are also cat ladies. The woman who watches our livestock when we go away on vacation is a big-time cat lady. There's even a cat lady who I've gotten to know at the ticket counter of our local US Airways terminal.

And, because I cannot tell a lie, I'll proudly admit at this time that even my wife is cat lady!

As a veterinarian, I occasionally ponder the question of why it is that otherwise normal wives, mothers, maiden aunts, and widows so often become cat ladies. The answer I always end up with is really quite simple: I don't know.

And the reason I don't know has to do with the large amount of diversity, both in the types and personalities of all of the cat ladies that exists out there in the world. And what I mean by this is that being a cat lady seems to indiscriminately include all of the age groups, all of the various levels of society, and includes, as well, the entire range of economic abilities. Also, the actual definition of what it takes to be a true cat lady is not precisely clear.

However, in an attempt to solve this mystery, I've narrowed down cat ladies into two broad categories: those women who have achieved cat-lady status on purpose, and those women who have had cat-lady status thrust upon them by fate.

With the first category of cat ladies, the answer is easy: they just plain love cats. They love being around cats. They love talking about cats, reading about cats, and hearing other people's stories about cats. They actively seek them out at animal shelters and in newspaper ads. They make a point of letting all of their friends, coworkers, and family know they love cats and will take all they can get. But even though, by my definition, these women are technically cat ladies, they are not what most people have in mind when they think of *real* cat ladies.

What most people think of when they think of cat ladies are mainly those who are in the second category; that is, women who've had the condition of cat-lady status thrust upon them by chance. With these precious women, the process of becoming a cat lady was generally a slow and subtle one. They didn't start out in life with the intention of becoming a cat lady; it was just something that happened. It seemed as if all of the cosmic forces that rule our infinite universe conspired to their having become so. The process often goes something like this.

The soon-to-be cat lady goes along quite happily for years with maybe two or three cats of her own when, out of nowhere, a stray kitty happens to show up on her back porch, always on the coldest, snowiest, or rainiest day of the year. And because she feels sorry for the poor, starving beast, the kind and nurturing animal lover starts to feed it. This homeless little orphan—who, without fail, somehow or another, always turns out to be a pregnant female—then decides in her little cat mind she really likes this nice lady's house, and so she then decides to stick around to give birth to her kittens.

From then on, it just keeps getting better. Because the kittens are (of course!) always super cute and adorable, the nice lady decides to keep just two of them. After all, what harm could there be in feeding a couple more mouths? And so she does. She manages to find another cat lady who then takes the extra kittens off her hands and keeps a boy and a girl for herself. She then dutifully has the mama cat spayed, and all is well. Or so she thought.

Because her budget was a little stressed with the extra feeding and veterinary care for the cherished new kittens, she cannot afford right away to have either of them fixed. And before she even knows what hit her, the young female and her male sibling soon began he'ing and she'ing, and now the little darling is pregnant. Before you know it, she's become a cat lady.

But it doesn't end there. Once word gets out that a person attains cat-lady status, these gentle souls then become easy victims to an endless deluge of additional unneeded cats. One of the largest of these sources—and also the most annoying—is from people who are supposedly her friends. These people, somehow or other, got stuck with either unwanted kittens (usually the result of them not having their own cat spayed), or an unneeded adult cat (which they've often just inherited from their mother-in-law).

Another dilemma that cat ladies have to deal with are perfect strangers who pawn off cats on them. It turns out that if a rare individual doesn't happen to know any cat ladies, they will, by hook or crook, skillfully seek one out.

First, they will ask their friends if they happen to know any cat ladies. Then, if this doesn't work, the more ambitious ones will just hang around grocery store checkout lines looking for women who are buying cat litter by the fifty-pound bag. If they're really desperate, they might even drive around their neighborhoods on recycling days, looking for the houses with the ten or more plastic bins full of empty cat food cans. They don't stop until they succeed.

Another phenomenon that seems to befall a person who achieves cat-lady prominence is what I refer to as the cosmic connection. Without getting too mystical about the whole thing, these accidental cat-lady types somehow or another always manage to find themselves wherever there are cats in distress.

For these ladies, what starts out as an innocent trip to a convenience store to buy a six-pack (of Mountain Dew, of course) always manages to turn into a lifesaving mission. This is because they mysteriously find themselves showing up at the store at just the same moment the store's manager happens to discover a litter of stray kittens in the Dumpster next to the building's parking lot.

Or she just happens to be driving home from church on Sunday morning (always on a cold and rainy Sunday morning!) and happens to spot an exhausted and near-death, abandoned cat in the middle of the road just seconds away from getting squashed by an eighteen-wheeler. Because she could no more leave this poor critter in the road any more than she could leave a child, she stops to rescue it.

She then drives like a maniac to her veterinarian's home (she feels her cat-lady status gives her the right to this lack of courtesy), and begs him/her to check the poor beast out.

The vet, who's always just on his or her way out the door for a precious afternoon outing with the family, tells her that with the exception of being slightly malnourished, the cat should do just fine. And yes—as is always the case—it's also pregnant. She promises the doctor she'll stop by tomorrow with the payment for his fee, takes the cat home, and nurses it back to health. Oh, and because they're so adorable, she keeps a few of the new mama's kittens.

Besides all of the above processes, which manage to keep cat ladies everywhere blessed with an endless supply of cats, there is one additional source that very few people ever consider. It revolves around a little-known fact that exists out there in the cat world: A cat, whether we like it or not, always chooses its owner.

Over the years, while helping out at our local SPCA, I've seen this curiosity take place firsthand. A dozen times I've watched hopeful future cat owners walk through the cat adoption area as they looked for their perfect new pet. In some cases, a particular cat will stay near the back of a cage and appear crabby and unsociable as an individual or family passes. When this happens, its my opinion that in this cat's little mind, he's decided he doesn't want to go home with these people and does what he can to be overlooked. Later in the hour, I've watched this same cat come dashing forward to the front of the cage, purring, floozying around, and looking all kinds of cute and adorable in an attempt to convince the folks looking at him to take him home. It's really quite amazing.

The same fact holds true for cats who already have a home. If, for whatever reason, they're not happy living where they are, they'll move on. As proof of this, all you have to do is look at the bulletin board in my clinic or the missing pet section of the local newspaper. There's always a ton of missing cats. Its my belief that, although a few may have fallen upon foul play, most of these missing cats were just out looking for a new home.

And it's here where the cat ladies come in. A lot of the cats that show up at their homes very likely did so because they were seeking a better place to live. Many of these strays that show up out of the blue were probably just passing by when they happened to notice all of the other happy and contented cats lying around. Anxious to find a good home, they probably said to themselves: *Hmm, this must be a great place to live. Look at all of those happy cats. I wonder if maybe I just show up on this lady's back porch and look hungry and tired, she'll feed me, too.* And she of course does; after all, what's one more mouth to feed?

I can hear it out there now: "So, Doc, this is all pretty interesting stuff. But just what are the rules concerning who is, or who is not, a cat lady?"

Good question! Over the years, I've checked out all of the books I could get my hands on, as well as spoken with many of the eminent authorities on the matter, and I have not been able to discover any reliable notion of precisely what a cat lady is. Therefore, I'm declaring myself an authority on the subject and hereby, for the first time in recorded history (at least that I know of), will establish the following official rules as they pertain to being a bona fide cat lady.

As I mentioned way back in the beginning of this story, even though cat ladies come in all sizes, shapes, ages, and socioeconomic backgrounds, they have to adhere firmly to two rules. The first rule is that in order to be a cat lady, you must be a woman; that is, a female human past the age of consent.

Hmm, I can almost hear some grumbling out there. In my defense, let me say that I don't insist that cat ladies be women because I'm a chauvinist pig or any of that other nonsense. I say it because, at least in my humble life's experience, I've never met or have ever known of or have ever even heard the term, *the cat man*—or, if you prefer, *the cat dude*.

(One possible exception to this rule could be the author Ernest Hemingway. For anyone who has ever visited his home in Key West, the first thing you'll notice is that there are about seventy cats running around it. Legend has it that all of these cats are all descended from a seven-toed calico female he'd won on a bet from a old Portuguese sea captain he'd met at Sloppy Joe's Bar. Whether he had that many cats while he was still alive forty years ago, I can't say for sure. One thing I do feel comfortable about saying is that as macho as he was, I don't think he'd like being referred to as a cat lady.)

Rule number two, although slightly less controversial, answers the big question: "So, Doc, how many cats do you need to have in order to make the leap from just a plain old cat lover to that of full-fledged cat lady?" Well, after years of study and observation, I've concluded that seven is the minimum number of cats needed in order to be an official cat lady.

Why seven? I'm not exactly sure. It possibly could be that seven is the number of cats that can be fed with one large-size bag of cat food in a week. Maybe its the number of cats needed to raise the cost of veterinary care into the budget category of a major household expense. Or, since I'm the one sticking my neck out and breaking new ground with the publication of this landmark thesis, it could just be that it's the number I like best.

There is a second part to this seven-cat rule that's also very important. It answers the question of what happens to a cat lady when her household's cat population drops below seven. What is she then, if all of her cats run away because she switched to a discount store's cat food brand in order to save a few bucks? What if a bad case of feline distemper slipped into the brood, and her population of cats drops down to two? What if the neighbor's rottweilers break through the screen door of her back porch while she was off buying cat litter and . . . ? I need say no more. Or, worst of all, what if because of her neighbor's incessant complaints about the repulsive smell permeating their community as the consequence of all her unneutered tomcats constantly having urinating contests results in her receiving a health department summons? And what if this summons results in her having to divest herself of all her animals?

My answer to these unfortunate events is this: Just like circumcision in men, being a cat lady is forever, even if you drop below seven cats. Why is this so? It's because in my experience, most of the time, this drop below the magic number of seven is just a temporary setback.

I know, a lot of former cat ladies may challenge this assertion and say, "Oh no! Never again, Doc, will I ever have that many cats; I've learned my lesson." But after a while, when they least expect it, they'll see one of those enticing cat food commercials that always come on during *The Judge Judy Show*; and before you can say "Fancy Feast," the old emotions will return.

The next day, they'll wake from a fitful night's sleep with an overpowering urge to visit their local SPCA. (Real cat ladies would NEVER think of buying a cat from a pet store.) Or they might start looking in the Dumpsters of the local Wal Mart or driving down lonely back country roads, just on the outside chance there might be an abandoned litter of kittens waiting to be saved.

And because everyone knows that once you're a cat lady, you're then a cat lady for life, some co-worker, friend, or maybe even a complete stranger will sense your need and provide you with a new little bundle of furry joy.

You know you can't escape it, so you just give in, and because you do, the world will be a better place. And besides, you can always tell yourself, "Hey, what's one more mouth to feed?"

CHAPTER SEVEN

MORE LOVE IN MY HEART

Back in the early days of my veterinary career when I still did a lot of dairy farm calls, one of the things that really smoked my drawers—that is, something that made me really angry—was the two-o'clock-in-the-morning phone call that, more often that I care to remember, often went something like this: "Doc," the farmer's wife would say, "my husband wanted me to call you and tell ya that Ol' Betsy has been trying to calve for some time now. But for some reason, she's havin' trouble getting the baby to come out. He wants to know if you would mind coming out to the farm and see if you can help her?"

After the usual couple of seconds of silence that I needed in order to collect myself from the stupor of just having woken up from a sound sleep, I'd mentally make a list of all of the reasons I had to get up and quickly respond to this call. I'd say to myself, "OK, Richard, this is a calving; this is a true medical emergency; this is extremely important to the client's livelihood; the sooner you get there, the greater the chance is of you saving this little guy."

At about this time, the wife would usually ask, "Hey Doc, are you still there?"

After a couple more seconds, I'd firmly tell myself, *OK, Richard, you better wake up. Now!*

"Yes, I'm still here," I'd reply, vigorously shaking my head in a further attempt to rouse myself. By this time, even though my body still resided in la la land, my mind would already be racing full speed ahead. Without having to even think about it, my brain would automatically size up the difficulty of the problem, the location of the farm, and the medical abilities of its owners. By the time my body finally caught up with my brain, I was ready to ask the ultimate question, the question that would tell me immediately whether this farm visit would go well or whether it would be a nightmare. "Ma'am," I'd calmly ask, "how long has the cow been in labor?"

In the case of the particular client above, I already had my suspicions as to what the answer would be.

After a couple of seconds of silence, she said, "Well, um, uh, Doc, let me think." I could tell from the slight trembling in her voice that she needed some time in order to build up her courage. "Oh, probably since about since about four o'clock yesterday afternoon, maybe five."

This was about six hours longer than they should have waited.

Son of a gun [those were not my exact words], I thought to myself, *I knew it. I just knew it!* And the reason I knew what the answer would be, before she even said a word, was because her husband had *her* make the phone call to me. He realized that if it was he who had called, I'd have jumped all over him and given him a strong piece of my mind for having waited so darned long before calling me.

Wide awake now, I did all I could to contain my wrath. Strongly resisting the temptation to ask her why in the heck they didn't call me sooner, I growled into the phone that I'd be there as soon as I could and slammed the receiver down.

The problem I had with this middle-of-the-night call, was not the fact that it occurred at two o'clock in the morning. These types of emergencies are to be expected because, whether you're a physician or a veterinarian, when mamma is ready to give birth, she's ready, regardless of the hour. No, what irritated me most about this type of call (and still irks me when it happens in my small animal practice) is that the client waited until the last possible minute before deciding to take any action.

And so, as I often do when this most frustrating type of emergency call comes in, I got myself up, and as I was getting dressed, I ranted and raved, and over and over again spewed out words I hadn't used since back my Navy days. My wife, who always had the misfortune of having to witness these tantrums, would calmly wait until I was done and then say to me, "Richard, now don't you forget that, back in the days when we were farmers, you used to have to make the very same phone call that this poor farmer just did. So try to be a little more understanding. You have to try to have a little more love in your heart."

With very few exceptions, having to deal with emergencies at all hours of the day and night is one of the least welcome aspects of a doctor's job description. And, unless you belong to a group practice in which all of the doctors can take turns, or unless you practice in a speciality such as dermatology or cosmetic surgery, there's really no way of avoiding them.

My personal feelings with regards to emergencies are quite complicated. On one hand, emergency calls, because of their often extreme and critical nature, give me the opportunity to apply many exciting medical procedures and techniques which, in the course of normal day-to-day operations, I would rarely get to employ. Also, the caring and dedication I demonstrate by responding to the need of emergency care reinforces the bond between my clients and me and gives me a chance to really shine.

On the other hand, responding to emergencies at all hours of the day and night is more often than not one of the biggest sources of frustration in this business that I have to deal with, and these frustrations ruthlessly take their toll. First off, at least in my rural practice, two of the most common emergencies I see are what we vets call HBCs (hit by cars) and BD/LD injuries (big dog/little dog fights). Both HBCs and BD/LD injuries nearly always present with gruesome damage as well as a huge amount of pain on the part of the victim. The owners, because of the unexpected nature of the whole situation, are frequently in a state of profound mental anguish and are very difficult to deal with. And, sadly, most of these emergencies often end tragically with the death of the pet.

The second big problem with emergencies is of a more personal nature. There are the missed—or interrupted—theater performances, the unforgivable need of having to leave early—or not being able to attend at all—family Thanksgiving and Easter dinners, the unwelcome violations of the sanctity of one's toilet time, as well as the invasions of privacy during quiet moments with my wife.

And worse than any of these is the proven scientific fact that every time the phone rings at two o'clock in the morning and cuts short a much-needed good night's sleep, my life expectancy is probably shortened by about a week.

But all in all, most of the time it doesn't really bother me all that much. I just do it and don't think about it. Like firemen, ambulance drivers, hospital emergency room staff, furnace repairmen, and tow-truck drivers, I do it because it's what I've chosen to do, and I can't imagine life any other way.

In my years of being in this business of veterinary medicine, I think I've probably seen every type of human temperament and response there is to be seen with regards to pet owners, their pets, and emergencies. I've classified these emergency calls into four basic types: the true emergency types, the panic types, the inconsiderate/thoughtless types, and the infamous wait-until-the-last-minute types.

The true emergency types, fortunately, are my least frequently encountered emergency. These calls rarely cause me any grief because they're always genuine. The true emergency types are clients who have taken a second, amid their chaos, to calmly and rationally think about whether or not their pet's emergency really requires them to make that middle-of-the-night phone call to the vet.

Most of the time their decision is fairly straight-forward: the pet's muzzle and throat are swollen to three times their normal size due to an allergic re-action from a bee sting, and the poor critter can no longer breathe; the dog is not moving its hind end as the result of being just run over by a pickup truck; the pet's front leg is just dangling by a piece of skin from its body because of a gunshot wound; and on and on. All of these are true emergencies.

The second type of emergency calls I get are what I refer to as the panic type. Just like swatting at a fly who has landed on your potato salad, or reach-ing for the knob on the car's radio to turn up the volume when a favorite song comes on, these lov-ing and concerned pet owners' first reaction is not one of thought or consideration but that of reflex.

Their dog returns to the house from its evening bowel movement outside with slight limp and it's, "Quick, we gotta call the vet!" Another common example—and one that seems to strike blind terror in the hearts of many owners—is the cat who's just come back from a day's outing and has a tapeworm on the fur under its tail. Even though it's midnight (always on a Saturday or Sunday), the owner's knee-jerk response is, "Yuck, we'd better tell the vet. Now!"

Likewise, there are the borderline panic cases in which the owner calls to tell me that he has just returned home to discover his Labrador has just downed a one-pound bag of Hershey's Kisses, plastic bag, aluminum foil, and all; there are the slightly embarrassed calls worrying about a ravenous little dachshund who just gulped down several of the owner's birth control pills; and, though less common these days, there is still the occasional anonymous call from an owner worrying about their killer pit bull who has consumed a fresh batch of marijuana-laced brownies.

Another frequent panic/hysterical type of call I receive—also, always between the hours of midnight and two A.M.—involves having to instruct clients who have just cut their dog's toenails too close on how to get them to stop bleeding. (Someday, before I pass on into the big veterinary hospital in the sky, I'm going to do a study of just what it is that motivates some people to wait until midnight to clip their dog's nails.)

As cynical as I may perhaps sound about all of these calls, most of the time I honestly don't mind them too awfully much, because they usually can be taken care of over the phone or at worst, be delayed until morning. These calls can also be quite humorous.

The next type of emergency calls I get are the ones that really make me want to run off to that South Pacific island I often fantasize about and spend the rest of my days painting pictures of scantily clad natives. I mean, these are the calls that *really* get me mad. I label these callers the inconsiderate or completely thoughtless type. And, unfortunately for us veterinarians, these callers are more common than the average person would believe.

There's the lady who calls just past midnight to ask me what my office hours are; there's the guy who has an uncontrollable need to tell me his dog has just vomited up what looks like maggot-infested woodchuck parts; there is the girl who calls and wants to know what's the best shampoo to use to bathe her cat; or there's the person who wants to know where he can find a home for his dalmatian who has just bitten a jogger.

These calls kill me! And even though I don't have to get up, dress, and go in to the office, I'll often lie in bed seething for hours, as I try to figure out and come to terms with just how these people could be so thoughtless.

The last type of emergency call I get, although not quite as irritating as the inconsiderate types just mentioned, are still some of the most frustrating cases I have to deal with. I call these folks the wait-till-the-last-minute types. These are clients who wait until the last possible minute—usually about midnight on the Saturday of a long holiday weekend—before seeking medical help for their animal.

There are many reasons people wait until the last minute. One of the most common involves the universal human hope that a miracle will occur and the problem, if given enough time, will just go away. Sometimes an owner's reason for delay is that they just simply didn't realize the severity of their pet's problem. All is well and good until a friend or family member stops by for a visit and creates a feeling of guilt or points out a need for a call to action.

However, at least from my experience, most of the time, the answer as to why these procrastinating owners wait so long in dealing with their pet's problem is simply one of neglect or just plain laziness. There is the old Labrador who's had difficulty getting up or down for the last two months, and now, suddenly (?), he can't move his hind legs; the cat whose breathing has been rapid and strained for the past week and who now has its tongue hanging out of its mouth and is turning purple; or there's the six-month-old, unvaccinated, unwormed rottweiler who's been constantly vomiting for two days and is now crapping himself to death from parvovirus because its owner chose to ignore getting the dog its shots.

The two biggest problems I have with these wait-till-the-last-minute types are first, I have to get up and drive in to the office, only to find most of these guys dead on arrival or too far gone to save. It's awfully depressing, and I absolutely hate it. The second problem is often, despite my heroic efforts and great expense, there is a greater than fifty percent chance I won't be paid.

Over the years, I've stopped asking these procrastinating owners why they ever waited so long before they brought their pet in; it just made them feel even more guilty than they were before I asked the question. But more importantly—at least from my point of view—I stopped asking why because having to listen to these owners' pathetic whining and lame excuses just plain pissed me off worse. I know, I know, my wife tells me I have to have more love in my heart; and I try. And I'll keep on trying, but sometimes, it is oh so hard.

CHAPTER EIGHT

PONDERING THE MEDICAL MYSTERIES

A few years ago, I received a letter from my good friend and colleague, Dr. Steve. I remember that as I pulled it from my mailbox, the first thing I noticed as I examined the front of the envelope was that it had been sent from the country of Ecuador. "That's where I really want to go," I remembered him saying to me time and time again during our many conversations together while still at school. "I just know I can do some good there." And as I opened the letter and began to read it, I was overjoyed to learn his precious dream had, indeed, come true.

Steve and I were classmates together at vet school. After graduation, as all of my other colleagues and I were heading out into the business world (we now had to make the past eight years of college pay off), Steve joined the Peace Corps. Even though he'd been medically trained to care for and treat animals, his ultimate goal in life was to help end all human suffering. My opinion then—and is to this very day as well—is that the farmers and villagers of that faraway, remote region in the high Andes Mountains were blessed to have him, not just because he was a talented vet but because he's a gentle and compassionate human being as well.

In his letter, Steve talked at great length about the breathtaking mountain scenery of his new home and of the many customs and fascinating traditions of his beloved clients; he spoke in great detail about the not so well-known fact that guinea pigs are considered a delicacy; and he spoke with great admiration of the local parish priest, a Frenchman, who loved to drink Jack Daniel's whiskey.

He also spoke of the many interesting cases he'd been called out on and had managed to resolve: a blood disorder in cattle that occurred every year, which was the result of them eating bracken fern; chronic salt and mineral deficiencies, which he helped to remedy by founding and helping to build a small-scale salt-block manufacturing industry; and how he would organize seminars in the surrounding villages in order to teach his clients the about the most basic of animal husbandry techniques such as worming, parasite control, and selective breeding.

One particular story Steve recounted in his letter struck me as particularly interesting. It highlighted to me, in the simplest of terms, a universal human behavior that exists not only in the high mountains of Ecuador but in our modern and highly educated culture as well. It's a behavior that I, as a veterinarian, have to do battle against nearly every day: that is, the relentless war against folk cures and home remedies.

Steve had been called out to a small family dairy farm to examine a cow that had a severe and chronic case of diarrhea. Because his workload was so large (at the time he was the only veterinarian for hundreds of miles around) he was not able to answer the call until later the next day. When he finally did arrive at the farm and started examining the cow, the very first thing he noticed was that her right ear had a big, blood-soaked bandage on it. He also discovered that the cow no longer had diarrhea. With the problem having already been solved, he then became curious about the poor cow's ear. Thinking that maybe the critter had been attacked by dogs or maybe had just gotten her head struck in her stall, he casually asked the farmer about the bandaged ear.

The farmer told Steve of a neighbor of his who had some talent as a medicine man. Worried about his cow becoming dehydrated by its diarrhea, he called on this neighbor to come to his farm. The neighbor/medicine man, after performing an elaborate ritual of chanting and tossing a copper coin over the cow's back in an attempt to discover the cause of its illness, then grabbed the poor beast by its right ear and made three big slices in it with his machete.

Steve was absolutely stunned when the farmer told him this; he couldn't in his wildest dreams believe anybody would ever do such a foolish thing. After taking a couple of seconds in order to calm down, he asked the farmer why he would let this neighbor do such a ghastly thing to his treasured milk cow. The farmer, as if it was the most natural thing in the world to make three bloody gashes in a cow's ear with a machete, calmly told Steve that the medicine man had to do what he did in order to let the "bad blood" out of the cow; this, in turn, would cure the diarrhea. Steve concluded the story by speculating that, whether modern medicine likes it or not, this example of "medicine by machete" he'd witnessed did seem to work. At least on this particular cow.

Now, I'm sure that all of you out there reading this are thinking to yourselves, *Ya know Doc, cutting three deep gashes into one's pet's ear with a sharp pocket knife in order to cure its diarrhea sounds like a very strange thing to do.* And, of course, you'd be absolutely right! But as bizarre as this so-called cure for diarrhea may sound to us, we, in our modern and highly enlightened society, are equally guilty of some pretty outlandish—and, quite often, deadly— non-medical therapies.

Before I begin to give a few examples of some weird modes of treating diseases that I've had the opportunity to have been involved with, I'll start by admitting to all the world that I understand why we turn to such procedures. From all of my humble dealings with my fellow man, I know that somewhere, deep, deep, within us human beings, there exists this innate, almost instinctual compulsion, that whenever we have a health problem, be it medical, physical, emotional, or spiritual, we *must* take a pill, we *must* drink a potion, slap on a poultice, or perform some ancient healing ritual. We just can't help ourselves. Its in our nature.

As I mentioned earlier, one of the biggest battles I must wage in my day-to-day practice of veterinary medicine (and my human counterparts probably must deal with it as well) is that of dealing with the ineffectiveness—and very often, the serious consequences as well—of clients' home remedies with regards to self-medicating their pets. And believe me, I've seen some real doozies. The biggest area in which the home remedies business is alive and well is that of flea control.

Two of the most common home remedies for the treatment/prevention of fleas, which I'm asked about daily, are brewer's yeast and garlic. Many of my clients swear by the effectiveness of these two products. If you walk into any larger pet store, you'll see about a billion products for sale that combine one or both of these ingredients. Year after year, I patiently listen to the endless testimonials of the greatness of these natural, almost miraculous flea control products.

And the reason I listen so patiently is twofold: the first is that these two products essentially do no harm. Brewer's yeast is actually an excellent source of B vitamins. The second is that I know, if given enough time, all of these brewer's yeast enthusiasts will eventually ask this question: "Doc, I just don't understand it. I've been feeding this brewer's yeast/garlic for years. But for some reason, it just ain't workin' this year. Do you think maybe I got a bad batch? How come it isn't working?"

The answer I always give (and I wish I had a dollar for every time I've had to give this explanation) to these poor, despondent pet owners is that there exists no scientific evidence or controlled clinical trials, whatsoever, to show that these food products work at all. Absolutely none.

Then, after waiting a couple of seconds for this bad news to sink in, I say that there is nothing inherent, either physically or chemically, in these two ingredients that would keep away or kill fleas. I tell them that it was very likely that the remedy worked so well for them in the past because they had no fleas to begin with.

In the category of the "most stupid" alternative flea control product I've had the displeasure of dealing with would be that of a former client who called me one Sunday morning because his little female beagle hound was seizuring. He said that he'd just given her a sponge bath with gasoline to get rid of her fleas. The unfortunate little creature was dead before she arrived at the office. And believe me, this ignoramus caught an earful of my wrath; hence the reason he's now an ex-client.

Other equally foolish—but not quite as deadly—home treatments for fleas I've seen or have heard about are: dusting the poor beasts with fireplace ashes, spritzing the unfortunate critters with kerosene, rubbing the dog down with used motor oil, powdering the pet from head to toe with baking soda, and saturating it with tea tree oil. Although most of these products will, indeed, kill fleas, they all potentially can cause digestive upsets, blindness, mechanical pneumonia, or severe skin rashes, blistering, and chemical burns, not to mention a great deal of pain as well. They should not even be considered.

Another method told to me by an old, tobacco chewin' woodsman surely would win the prize in the category of "most gross." He told me that every summer, he'd concoct a poultice out of the wads of chewed-up tobacco and gobs of spit juice that he accumulated especially for this task. He would then rub it into his poor hound dog's coat. Ummmm, yummy.

And topping off my list of unusual flea control products would be the aromatherapy necklaces. Although most owners create their own secret blends, some of the ingredients I've gotten them to divulge are: ponderosa pine tree bark, dried citrus potpourri, and my all-time favorite, herbal essence of wood nymph, whatever that is. Do these fragrant necklaces work? I'm not sure, but I will say this: They sure smell nice.

Another area in which folk cures and the home remedy arts are practiced with great flourish is in the area of tick control and removal. The tick control part mirrors that of the previously discussed flea control, and I won't discuss it any further.

Where the real hocus-pocus comes into play is the art of tick removal.

In my practice, it seems that for every intact and whole tick a client brings their pet in for me to remove, there are another five pets brought in for me to treat with the tick already dead, mangled, or decapitated. (Ticks, by definition, don't have heads; they have a capitulum.)

I've seen ticks painted with passionate pink nail polish as well as coated with nail polish remover. I've seen ticks with their rear ends blackened by a cigarette, and others that have been literally blown to bits by a burning match. I've seen them doused with olive oil, mineral oil, kerosene, rubbing alcohol, vodka, Jack Daniel's whiskey, flea spray, Tabasco sauce, gasoline, and yes, even my old friend, udder balm. None of these substances work with any predictable success. All they do is kill the tick. And it must be remembered that if you kill the tick while it's still attached, it can no longer open its mouth parts. If the poor critter can't open its mouth, then when you go to pull it out, you'll end up with the tick's body between your fingers (or tweezers), and its head now firmly embedded in your pet.

Speaking of udder balm, here's a product that is probably misused—with the possible exception of aspirin—more than any other that I see. Before I start ranting, let me just say that udder balm is a fantastic salve. For nonfarm readers who may not know anything about udder balm, it is a thick, lanolin-based goop that, when used as directed, brings blessed relief to dried, chapped, and sunburnt cow udders. When my wife and I were dairy farmers, we used the stuff all of the time. It's a marvelous product.

But, having said that, I'll now state that it is my sincere opinion (and, again, this is my opinion only) that the second to the lowest levels of Dante's hell should be reserved exclusively for pet owners who use this product indiscriminately on their cats or dogs. Maybe that's a little strong, but it's just about the way I feel.

I've seen the sticky substance slathered over the entire backs of dogs, like hickory barbeque sauce on a slab of baby back ribs, for the sole purpose of treating fleas. I've seen it used in a futile attempt to cure mange around a dog's eyes, to treat gunshot wounds, and to attempt to cure hot spots on golden retrievers. I've had clients who've gobbed the stuff into the pet's ears with the intention of treating yeast infections and another who massaged it onto a cat's leg that was contaminated with a draining, pus-filled, bite-wound abscess. I even had a client who tried to cure a cancerous ulcer on his pit bull's testicles with the product. I remember him lamenting to me, "Doc, I just don't understand it! The SOB tries to bite my hand off every time I rub the stuff on him. Doc, do you think it burns or something?" I told him that I didn't know the answer to that question. (I resisted the temptation to tell this guy to perhaps massage some of the udder balm onto his own testicles and see for himself why the dog didn't like it.)

I could go on and on discussing alternative cures and remedies that I've seen and heard of to treat everything from worms and diarrhea to saggy ears and arthritis. But I'll end by telling one last true cow story from my own experience.

I'd gotten called out to a dairy farm to look at a Holstein heifer (For my nonfarm readers, a heifer is a cow who's going to have a baby for the first time) who, because of having given birth to an oversized calf, had some sort of nerve damage to her hind legs and could no longer stand up. This is a particularly severe problem for a milk cow because they have such a heavy body that when they're down for too long a time in one position and can't get up, the muscles in the down-side leg start to cramp up and die because of poor blood circulation. It is, therefore, very important to get the cow standing as soon as possible.

After examining the cow for any obvious internal damage, I gave it a few drugs to relieve any inflammation in its muscles or spinal cord, helped the farmer and his sons roll the cow over onto its other side, and left some additional drugs with the farmer to be given later. I left instructions to turn the cow every two hours and said I'd try to stop back the next morning. I then left to go to my other afternoon appointments.

The next morning, I happened to be driving by the farm with this downed cow and stopped for a second to see how she was doing. I expected her to be up and perhaps even in the milking barn. She wasn't. I could see where the poor beast had dragged herself all over the box stall in a futile attempt to rise, but she just couldn't get the muscle strength or coordination to do so. This was not a good sign.

I examined the cow again, gave her a few more drugs, and left instructions with the farmer to keep turning the cow. I stopped back twice more that day to check on the progress of the cow. She still had not gotten up.

When I stopped the next day to check on the cow, the poor girl, despite the fact that she was eating and drinking just fine, still could not get her legs under herself to stand. My experience was that when a cow had been down this long, it was very likely it would never stand again. I told this to the farmer and suggested that he might at least salvage some of his investment in her by butchering her and putting the meat into the freezer.

I hated saying this to the farmer because, first of all, he'd just spent two years raising this cow from a baby, and second, it's always quite a financial loss. A milk cow is worth three to four times the value of any beef he might get from her. I left the decision up to him. After a couple of seconds' thought, he told me he really liked this little heifer and that he wanted to give her every chance he could before putting her down. I said OK and told him I'd stop by if I was in the area.

Chance would have it that I was in the area the next day. As I walked into the box stall where the cow was, I was immediately struck with the distinctive odor of strong mustard. It was weird. Walking over to the still-down cow, I saw that her hipbones had been thickly coated with French's mustard. I scratched my head and started laughing out loud. A second later, the farmer walked in.

"Levi," I said to him, trying to be as serious as I could, "what the heck are you doing to this poor cow? I've never seen anything like this in my life." Looking at me as if it was the most natural thing in the world to spread mustard onto the hipbones of a living cow, he went on to tell me about a call he'd made to his cousin down in Pennsylvania.

"My cousin told me about the time he'd once had a down cow that his vet just couldn't get to stand up. He said that he called their uncle, who'd been in the dairy business for all of the eighty-some years of his life, and he told him to put a poultice of mustard over the cow's hipbones. My cousin said it worked great; the cow got right up the next day." Pointing to the two empty gallon jugs of French's mustard in the corner of the stall, he continued, "I couldn't get a hold of any mustard poultices, so I figured this store-bought stuff would be the next best thing."

I held back any urge I may have been harboring to make fun of this foolish method of treating his cow; I had too much respect for him and his family to embarrass him with any of the cynical comments I may have had on my mind. And so I just smiled and told him that his mustard therapy would probably do no harm. I then added, "Just in case, however, it doesn't work, keep rolling the cow to its opposite side every few hours. I'm almost positive she'll never get up because her poor leg muscles after all of this time are probably cramped up." I told him I would stop again the next time I was in the area.

But it was several days before I got back up to the farmer's dairy, and I'd forgotten all about his cow. When at last I got called by him to look at another one of his cows that had a sore foot, I asked him how he made out with the crippled cow. He looked at me, and smiling from ear to ear, said, "Doc, that's her over there; we've been milking her for a couple of days now. She turned out to be a great little milk cow. I'm sure glad we didn't put her in the freezer."

And sure enough, there she was, standing right up in her stall like nothing was ever wrong with her. She even still had the gobbed-up mustard on her backside. I couldn't believe it! I just stood there in absolute silence. I could only wonder what in the heck was going on.

"Yup, Doc," said the farmer. "That mustard sure did the trick. My cousin from Pennsylvania says it works every time."

I couldn't have agreed with him more.

CHAPTER NINE

AN EVENING AT HOOTERS

One Saturday afternoon after office hours, Theresa and I got into our old family Buick and drove out to a large mall located in a nearby city. Although neither of us are all that keen on shopping (or the maddening hordes of people that go with it), we make a point of trying to visit this particular mall a couple of times a year, just so we can see what's new out there in the world. I usually end up buying a couple of pounds of exotic coffee from the Vermont Coffee Bean Company as well as a few new books from the Barnes & Noble superstore. Theresa, who's a lot easier to please than me, is content to bring home a sampling of assorted sweets from the Gertrude Hawks chocolate store.

On this particular evening, after finishing our stroll around the mall, we decided to have a nice, quiet, sit-down supper at one of the mall's many fine eating places. For no reason other than that both of us are amateur bird-watchers, we chose a restaurant called Hooters; we thought that maybe we'd see a few owls. Phew! Were we wrong!

Dining at Hooters turned out to be quite an interesting and pleasant experience. The restaurant had all of the qualities that one should expect to find in a good eatery: excellent and very attentive service, delicious food, large portions, wholesome and healthy American girls tastefully dressed in a manner that profoundly emphasized their physical assets (maybe assets is the wrong word to use here), as well as very reasonable prices.

What a country! was all I could think to myself as we sat there enjoying our meal. They were doing a huge stroke of business; the place was packed to the walls. And as I sat there watching those Hooter ladies running themselves ragged trying to keep up with all of their customers, I found myself wondering—as I'm prone to do in situations like that—about how it is that some people manage to come up with such great ideas and then have the boldness and skill to pull it all off. It was really all pretty amazing.

We were a little disappointed, however, because we didn't see any owls. As a matter of fact, the closest thing to a bird of any kind that we saw were the medium-hot chicken wings I'd ordered as an appetizer. I guess the entrepreneurs and designers who'd thought up the theme for this particular restaurant had a slightly different concept in their minds when they decided to call their business Hooters.

And I can almost hear it out there now: "OK, Doc, so you and your wife took a walk on the wild side and had a nice supper at a Hooters restaurant. What's that got to do with veterinary medicine?"

As Theresa and I sat there enjoying our meal, we found ourselves watching with great interest—and quite a bit of fun—all of the various types and styles of mating rituals that many of the single young and middle-aged male patrons were performing for the benefit of all of those lovely Hooter ladies. I remember Theresa saying to me that seeing all of those guys maneuvering about crowing and strutting their stuff reminded her of a gaggle of love-crazed, barnyard roosters. I agreed.

But as time went on, somehow or other, the topic of our conversation turned to that of a rather frustrating discussion I'd had earlier in the day with a veterinary client of mine, who I'll call Bob. (Yes, as hard as we try not to, we still end up discussing our vet business, even during our time off.) The problem I had earlier in the day with Bob all revolved around a question that he sort of dropped upon me unexpectedly, for which I was completely at a loss to answer. That is, until Theresa's and my most-excellent dinner together at Hooters.

My friend Bob has been a client of my vet practice almost since the first day I hung up my shingle. He's a big man, an old farm boy, a strong silent type of guy who possesses what I feel is a rare quality seldom seen in today's fast-paced society. That is, he practices the arts of respectful listening and deliberate thinking before he speaks.

During one of our first office visits together, Bob had brought in a very sick elderly cat for me to examine. She was about eighteen years old and was suffering from all of the effects of kidney failure: dehydration, muscle wasting, and foul breath. As I related these observations to Bob, all he did was stand across the table from me, staring and not saying a word. This behavior kept on for several minutes until I couldn't take it anymore. "Sir," I said, "is what I'm saying to you making any sense?"

Bob smiled, chuckled to himself a bit, and said, "People ask me that all of the time. I guess it gets on some people's nerves. He paused for a couple of seconds before continuing. "Doc," he said, "the reason our Lord gave us two ears and only one mouth was because he wants us to listen at least twice as much as we speak. When I talk, the only thing I can tell you is what I already know. That's it! I decided early on in my life that if I ever wanted to learn anything in this world, I would need to listen!"

I thought to myself at the time (and I still do) that this was quite a profound statement. But I have to admit that, until Bob told me this, his silence and attentive stare, were a little bit disconcerting. This was because, as a medical professional who often has to struggle to get a point across to anxious pet owners, I'd grown to rely on my clients interrupting me with their spontaneous questions or comments in order to give me some kind of feedback as to whether or not what I saying was getting through.

I explained to Bob that in this business, I often have to sum up complex medical philosophies and terms, which took me eight years of college to learn, into concepts and words that a client can understand. It's not easy, and despite doing my very best not to, occasionally a few lofty words slip in. And when this happens, I'd prefer to know at that moment, rather than have the client completely baffled by the time I've finished my explanation.

Bob smiled and said, "Don't worry, Doc, if what you were telling me made no sense, I'd be the first to let you know."

I thanked him for his honesty and directness.

Back to Hooters and our conversation about Bob. Bob had brought another of his cats in to the vet clinic earlier in the afternoon for the simple purpose of catching up on her shots. As I was examining the cat and getting the vaccines prepared, he and I talked about the usual things that guys talk about whenever they get a chance to do so: stuff like politics, the stock market, the weather, more politics, the condition of the county highways, etc. All was going along fine until Bob asked me a question that, when all was said and done, I couldn't answer.

He started out by innocently mentioning to me that he was a little worried about his female Labrador, Rosie, who I had spayed several months earlier. He said that she was gaining an awfully large amount of weight, and he was concerned about the effect it would have on her heart and hip dysplasia. "Doc," he said, "I just knew this would happen. Dogs always get fat after you fix 'em. Why is that, Doc?"

Bob's innocent comment-turned-question about dogs gaining weight after spaying or neutering is one I hear at least once a week. The answer I gave him was the same one I've given a thousand times before. "Bob, I hear that all of the time! All of this nonsense about animals gaining weight after getting spayed or neutered just isn't true. Over the course of a week here in this clinic, I see all kinds and shapes of dogs: fat spayed dogs, skinny spayed dogs, skinny neutered dogs, fat neutered dogs. Believe me when I tell you that it's just an old wives' tale."

After I finished speaking, I looked up at Bob, and I could tell by the disconcerted look on his face that what I had just said to him didn't quite fit into his life experiences on the matter. I think that had he been less of a gentleman, he probably would have told me I was full of crap.

I waited until I'd finished giving the cat her shots and put her back into her carrier before I continued. "Bob," I said, "I can tell by the look in your face that you don't believe me.

"Doc, its not that I don't believe you; it just seems like every dog or cat I get fixed gets fat as a hog."

"Bob, there is not a bit of scientific proof that fixing your pet has any effect whatsoever on their body weight. Its a matter of genetics and lifestyle. If your genes say that you're going to be heavy, and you're not careful with your diet and exercise, you'll gain weight." Confident that this explanation would get the point across, I concluded by saying, "If you're gonna gain weight, you'll do so whether or not you have your uterus and ovaries or testicles."

But Bob persisted; he wasn't gonna let me off the hook without a fight. "Doc, if that's the case, then why is Rosie gaining weight? I haven't been feeding her any more than I did before, and she still has the full run of the farm, so she still gets lots of exercise."

I looked at Bob, and he looked at me, and I realized that I was gonna have to bring out the big guns. "Bob, most people have their pets spayed or neutered right around the age at which the animal reaches puberty and young adulthood; that is, at about six months to a year of age. It just so happens that it is precisely at this time in an animal's life that mother nature directs their bodies to change from a strategy of growth to one that accumulates large amounts of subcutaneous adipose tissue (fat). Nature wants animals—and us—to have a little reserved body fat to carry them through potentially lean times. In females, especially, it's important to have a reserve of body fat in order to nurse any offspring they may have."

To further drive the point home, I gave myself as a perfect example. I told Bob about how I, at the tender age of twenty-two, as a young adult, had mustered out of the Navy, a slim and trim 135 pounds. And even though I'm not neutered, over the next several years, as I aged into adulthood, middle-age spread occurred, and I blossomed into the portly fellow I am today. (I didn't mention that the heavenly joys of marriage and the contentment of domestic bliss probably had as much to do with it as anything else.)

I assured him again. "Bob, the whole point is that if an animal or person's genetics says they're going to gain weight in their adulthood, they will do so (unless they're extremely careful) whether they have their ovaries or testicles or not."

Feeling pretty good with myself that I effectively shattered his false notion that young animals always gain weight after spaying or neutering, I looked over at Bob and saw he had a big smile on his face. Little did I know that he was about to blow my argument out of the water and just couldn't wait to begin.

"But Doc," he said, "don't you remember? She was already eight years old when you spayed her. She's quite an old lady. If, according to your argument, she was going to get fat as soon as she reached middle age, why didn't she get fat sooner?"

"Poop," I whispered to myself [poop was not the exact word I used]. I had forgotten about Rosie being an old dog. Completely baffled, I had to admit to Bob that I had absolutely no clue.

That is, until my wife and I went to Hooters. And before I go any further, I have to give full credit to Theresa for pointing out to me the obvious answer. Sitting there in the Hooters restaurant, surrounded by those masses of hormone-overloaded young males, all of whom were eating their hot chicken wings, drinking their beer, and ogling the young, healthy, asset-accentuated female waitresses, the answer to Bob's question as to why his eight-year-old Labrador gained so much weight after being spayed became obvious. As we both sat there watching those poor overworked girls running themselves ragged doing their job, while all the time having to put up with—and occasionally having to fight off—the amorous advances of their male customers, it all became perfectly obvious. As Theresa so vividly pointed out to me: "The old dog is gaining weight because she finally has some peace in her life. The poor girl no longer has to wear herself out running away from all of the horny boy dogs anymore."

CHAPTER TEN

JUST GOTTA KNOW

The wife: [in tears] "Doctor, Sweet Little Muffy (a long-haired, orange tiger cat) has been favorin' her left front paw for about three weeks now. My husband and I checked it out really close, and we can't find anything wrong. We want you to fix it."

The vet: [struggling to control Sweet (?) Little Muffy in order to give her a thorough exam] "No problem ma'am, I'll give her a good exam to see if I can find anything wrong just as soon as I get this wad of gobbed-up goop and hair that's stuck to her paw. What is this junk, anyway?"

The husband: [proudly] "We've been puttin' the old udder balm salve on it every couple of days, Doc. That stuff will cure anything!"

The vet: [looking up, slightly irritated, at the husband and wife as he struggled to clean the snarled-up, dirt and kitty litter—permeated blob of hair that used to be a cat's paw] "Why in the world did you put udder balm on it?"

The husband and wife: [together in harmony] "I don't know."

The vet: [after getting the paw clean] "It looks like a simple abscessed wound in between the toe pads. It's probably no big deal. I'll just clean it up real good and put Muffy on antibiotics. I'd also like you both to resist the temptation of putting any more udder balm on it."

The wife: [with a slightly perplexed look] "How do you think it could have happened, Doc?"

The vet: [smiling apprehensively, because he knew what was gonna happen next] "Ma'am, it appears to be a puncture wound of some sort, maybe from a nail or a thorn. We'll probably never know exactly what happened, nor does it really matter." [The vet wanted to nip the whole discussion in the bud before it got out of control.]

The husband: [equally bewildered and maybe even just slightly defensive] "No way, Doc. Sweet Little Muffy is too smart to do that, she would never step on a nail. It's gotta be something else!"

The wife: [in an equally huffy tone] "Yeah, Doc, no way would she ever step on a thorn. I know we got thorn apple trees out by the old barn, but she only goes there in the daylight."

The vet: [smiling, because, as he expected, the old round and round and round was about to begin, and there was no way in the world he was going to stop it] "A lot of times, these lesions could also be a simple bite wound from a mouse or mole."

The wife: [Her stern look and tightly pursed lips signaled to all present that this not knowing exactly what happened was starting to drive her crazy.] "No way, Doctor [with great emphasis] would our Sweet Little Muffy ever kill a mouse." [The vet chuckled to himself.]

The husband: [equally flustered by the whole situation] "Doc, do ya think she could have stepped on some broken glass? A few of years ago my brother-in-law got drunk and dropped a beer bottle out by the old outhouse."

The wife: [turning toward her husband with just a touch of rage] "My brother wasn't drunk; he just had one of his spells because he had too much to drink." [Turning toward the vet] "Doc, do you think Sweet Little Muffy could have stepped on an old toothpick? During our son's birthday party ten years ago, my mother-in-law insisted on throwing the toothpicks that held her martini olives onto the ground all over the yard. Do you think that's what happened?"

The vet: [enjoying this immensely] "I guess anything's possible." [He added, jokingly] "Maybe when that comet slammed into the planet Jupiter a few years ago, a sharp fragment flew off into space, then fell to earth, and Sweet Little Muffy just accidentally stepped on it."

The wife and husband: [staring at the vet in openmouthed disbelief] "Huh?"

The vet, seeing that his attempt at humor achieved nothing but scowling stares from the husband and wife, and knowing in his heart of hearts that this conversation would just go on and on and on, decided to bring out his famous secret strategy.

As a new veterinarian, just fresh out of vet school, and on my own in private practice, it didn't take me very long before I stumbled upon two monumentally important discoveries. In fact, the first discovery actually took place during my very first patient's visit in my brand-new clinic. The second discovery, which turned out to be even more important than the first, took about a week longer for me to finally understand. I would later call these two revelations, The First and Second Undeniable Truths of Veterinary Medicine. And although I didn't fully realize it at the time, these two absolute and immutable laws, in all of their infinite forms and degrees, would affect everything I'd do and say for the remainder of my professional life.

In moments of quiet reflection, when I look back on those chaotic and exhilarating early days of my new career, I remember that my discovery of these truths took me somewhat by surprise. Indeed, if I had to be perfectly honest, I was, at first, almost overwhelmed. However, when I finally calmed down and came to terms with them, I realized they wouldn't be all that bad to work with. I also came to the conclusion that perhaps if I'd paid just a little more attention in vet school, I would have seen them coming, and I might have been a little better prepared.

During those grueling years of trials and tribulations in my quest to become a veterinarian, there were the occasional subtle hints, the vague insinuations, which suggested to my beloved classmates and me the existence of these two problems. These rumors and hearsay would then be discussed and debated—always in hushed and reverent whispers—among ourselves during the rare, quiet moments in the anatomy laboratory or in the dark and distant lonely hospital corridors. The facts were staring us in the face, but none of us dared to admit it.

Also, to the best of my knowledge, not one of us lowly students dared to approach any of our cherished professors for the purpose of sharing our feelings with regards to these mysteries; because to us pilgrims, it all seemed just too bizarre to be true, and none of us wanted to be embarrassed. Likewise, for reasons known only to themselves, none of these kind doctors ever brought the subjects up. This reluctance on their part to say anything bothered me at first. But my feeling now is that these master teachers, with all of their infinite wisdom, probably just felt it would be better for us students to discover these dilemmas on our own.

The First Undeniable Truth of Veterinary medicine is that, as doctors of veterinary medicine, our patients will never, ever, tell us, in words, what is wrong with them. They'll never tell us that all they have is a splitting headache and they just want to be left alone to rest; never will tough old Spike, the Pekingese, ever be able to tell his mommy that he wishes she'd occasionally tie up his topknot with a pink bow (instead of the usual blue bow) because the pink one not only goes better with his bulging red eyes, but it also would help him get in touch with his feminine side; nor will Little Angel, the Siamese, ever be able to tell her daddy to please take that smelly canned tuna, which he insists on giving her with every meal, and which she absolutely loathes, and carefully but thoroughly shove it up where the sun don't shine, and just give her plain old Meow Mix.

Of course, there will always be cats who now and then might snarl and slash at me if I accidentally rub a painful wound the wrong way. There will always be dogs who'll try their darnedest to bite my face off if I painfully tweak a strained muscle or a broken leg the wrong way. And there will even be the occasional cow who will bellow out—and try and give me a swift, roundhouse kick to the head—if I mishandle her bruised, stepped-on tit. But these would be the rare exceptions.

(I would later on learn of certain gifted people, most of whom are from California or the high mountains of New Mexico, who claimed an ability to talk to and become "one" with animals. But as of this writing, I've not had a need to consult with any of them.)

When I first discovered the fact that none of my patients were ever going to talk to me, my first thought was that maybe the animals coming into my clinic may have been stuck up or, perhaps, just a little bit snooty. I sort of expected this because I was, after all, the new doctor in town. But when I asked their owners about the possibility of their little kitties or doggies being that way, I was assured—in no uncertain terms—this was not the case; no pets of theirs would ever act like that.

Then I thought that maybe they didn't speak the same language I did. Since I'd learned a little French in high school many years ago, I tried laying a few *"parlez vous Francais?"* on them. This question brought absolutely no response. Undaunted, I rushed down to the nearest Barnes & Noble superstore and purchased several different foreign phrase dictionaries. But this, too, was to no avail; neither Russian, Chinese, Arabic, Tagalog, nor Burmese would evoke a response.

Next, I came up with the thought that maybe all of my patients were deaf. Perhaps some bizarre experiment being performed at a U.S. Army base located twenty miles to the north of my practice had gone awry, causing all pets in my area to lose their hearing. Or maybe they could all hear, but because of some mysterious substance in the groundwater, they couldn't speak. To get to the bottom of this quandary, I performed a few medical tests—with the owners' permissions, of course—and came to the conclusion that neither of these possibilities were the answer to these mysteries.

Despite all of my efforts to do so, I just could not find any answer as to why my patients wouldn't talk, and if the truth were to be told, it drove me crazy!!! And so, in utter desperation, I gathered up my courage, got into my car, and decided to make a pilgrimage back to my revered veterinary college.

I'd made up my mind to go and ask the Master himself for a possible explanation to my predicament.

The Master, who has been teaching young skulls full of mush the noble art of veterinary medicine since the days of Noah and the ark, held court in his office next to the dairy barn every weekday afternoon but Thursday.

After arriving on campus, and as I found myself standing at the door to his office, I was suddenly overcome by a great fear; for several minutes, I wavered as to whether or not I should continue. But after a short prayer in which I asked our precious Lord for the strength to carry on, I raised my hand and knocked upon the exalted threshold.

From deep within the hallowed chambers arose the Master's booming voice: "Come in, can't you see the damned door is open?" I beamed with relief because my prayer had been answered; the Big Guy was graciously going grant me an audience.

I walked through the door and found myself standing there on that sacred ground. And as I stood there, amid his entourage of coffee klatchers and hangers-on, he watched me for several seconds. When he was satisfied that I was worthy of his consideration, he spoke.

With the benevolence and tenderness of a cornered rattlesnake, he demanded, "What the heck's [heck was not the exact word he used] your problem, Orzeck?"

After a minute or so of sufficient adulation and praise, I said, "Master, I've come to you with a problem that's been driving me crazy. My sincerest hope is you have the answer." For a second, I found my-self again wavering; this whole subject of my patients not wanting to talk to me just seemed so overwhelming. But I was determined not to back down. I had to know!

And so, mustering up the remainder of what little courage I had left, I looked him in the eye and just asked the question outright: "Sir, why is it that none of my patients ever talk to me?"

A great hush settled over the assembled multi-tude. The chamber became so quiet you could have heard a cat walking on a feather pillow in the next town. Everyone present was in a silent state of dis-belief. It was my opinion then—and it still is to this very day—that in the whole history of the human race, there had never been a new veterinarian who'd ever dared ask this question in such a direct man-ner.

A couple of seconds passed—it may have even been a couple of hours for all I know— before the Master spoke. With the loving compassion of a starv-ing she-lion ripping into the hind-quarter flesh of an African gazelle, he looked me square in the eye and let me have it with both barrels: "Orzeck, are you mentally impaired in some way? Of course, your darned [darned is not the exact word he used] pa-tients aren't going to talk to you. They're animals, and animals don't talk." And that was that.

The second discovery I made as a new veteri-narian was the existence of an insatiable, unrelenting, and seemingly uncontrollable human need to know why or how something happens: "Doc, why did my young kitty get kidney cancer?" "Richard, why did my dog get hip dysplasia?" "Sir, why did my old Siamese get a bladder infection?" "Why does my expensive purebred Lhasa apso have only one testicle?" And on and on and on.

At first, when I encountered this phenomenon of my clients' overpowering need to know why or how (and until I learned better), I did my utmost to speculate on these questions as thoroughly as I could. I would go through exhaustive lists of every known cause or theory of their pet's particular disease or ailment I could remember in an effort to answer the client's concerns.

But I soon learned that carrying out such an extensive rehashing of medical facts and figures accomplished nothing more than just plain wearing me out. I'm dead serious when I say this: after two or three of these encounters in the course of an afternoon's office hours, I'd have to go home and take a nap. But the most frustrating thing about having to explain in great detail the infinite number of possible causes of their pet's ailments is that, most of the time, the owners just weren't listening. They didn't listen because ninety percent of the time, they had the cause already figured out in their minds.

I'd know this because, after having just spent ten minutes compassionately telling them what I thought the reasons were for their pet's malady, the client would then bombard me with questions like: "Doc, what you say could be so, but do you think it could have been our well water? When my husband is hungover, he always gets the runs if he drinks our water straight from the sink." "Doc, do you think it could have been the yellow dye #3 in his dog food? I saw something on Jerry Springer about a woman who went berserk after she ate some Christmas cookies with yellow dye # 3 in 'em." "Doc, do you think it could have been the fact that my nephew dropped him on his head when he was a pup? My cousin from Maine was dropped on his head when he was nine years old, and he ain't never quite been right." "Doc, do you think it had anything to do with her being born on a Friday during a full moon?" And on and on; around and around and around. Clients will drive themselves crazy trying to find out why or how something happened.

I still try my best to help my clients with their need to know a reason. But I don't let it wear me out like it did at first, because I've learned of a few techniques to prevent these question- and-answer sessions from getting out of control. I've also learned that most of the time, when you really get down to it, there never really is an answer. A lot of people don't like to hear that, but that's the way it is. But even with all of my medical expertise and experience in dealing with an owner's need to know, I still occasionally run into a client or family who insists on going back and forth, knocking themselves out with their questions. For these folks, I bring out my secret weapon response.

Getting back to the conversation.

The vet: [Seeing that his attempt at humor failed miserably and suspecting there were private family issues between this husband and wife that would best be brought up somewhere else besides his waiting room, he decided it was time for his secret weapon.] "Folks, I agree that all of your theories are quite possible. But I got a better idea; let's just ask the cat."

The husband and wife: [momentarily shocked out of their seething rage] "Huh?"

The vet: [again] "Since she's the only one who knows exactly what happened, let's ask Muffy."

The husband: [still in disbelief] "What do you mean, Doc?"

The wife: [likewise in doubt] "Yeah, Doc, what are you talking about?"

The vet: [lowering his head to the cat sitting apprehensively on the exam table and looking it directly in its eye] "Please, little kitty cat, tell us what happened." [And then he lowered his ear to Sweet Little Muffy's mouth, just in case she wanted to whisper her answer.]

Muffy: Blank stare and total silence.

The vet: [one more time, just to freak out the clients] "Sweet Little Muffy, please, for the sake of your mommy and daddy's peace of mind, tell us all what happened."

Muffy: Blank stare and silence. [She thought about taking a swipe at the vet's ear but graciously chose not to.]

The husband: [calmer now] "I get your point, Doc. Thanks."

The wife. [also calmed down] "Me, too, Doc. But I have to tell you something, you are really weird!"

CHAPTER ELEVEN

LIKE A BOX OF CHOCOLATES

My dear old friend and world-renowned philosopher, Mr. Forrest Gump, has—in my humble opinion—one of the most profound ways I've ever heard of summing up all of the joys and the sorrows and infinite complexities of this beautiful world in which we all live into short, one- or two-line sayings. One of the most famous of these goes as follows: "My mama says life is like a box of chocolates; ya never know what you're gonna get."

And ain't that the truth!

When I think about it, I guess the same thing can be said about this business of veterinary medicine. When a client brings their pet into the office, you never quite know what you're gonna get, especially with regards to the clients themselves.

With the pets, its usually quite straightforward: Sick animals, most of the time, look and act sick. More importantly, we vets never have to worry about whether or not the pet is faking or has exaggerated its illness as our physician colleagues do. If an animal is good-natured and cheerful with all that life has to offer, we vets can pick up on this excitement immediately and use it to help strengthen our doctor/patient relationship. On the other hand, if the poor critter is scared, apprehensive, abused, or is just simply annoyed at the indignity of having to stand on my exam table, their low-level growl or quick slashing out of a paw toward my face will let me know that I'd better not get too chummy.

With their owners, however, it's a different story. Just like Mama Gump's proverbial box of chocolates, you never know what you're gonna get. Fortunately, in my experience, most clients turn out to be something like milk chocolate—covered buttercream-filled delights, just as sweet and smooth as can be and simply a joy to encounter. Some clients are like vanilla taffy or caramel nougat, a little thick and tough to chew on sometimes, but sweet and amiable nonetheless. Often, many clients are of an exotic flavor like coconut or mocha cream, different in their own special way, agreeable to work with, and always with an exciting story to tell.

Once in a while there are the occasional chocolate-covered nuts. (No! I'm not gonna go there.) And finally, you get stuck with the rare (thankfully) piece of pure dark, bitter, chocolate: the client who is impossible to deal with, who leaves a nasty taste in your mouth when they're gone, and who you wish, with all your heart, never walked through your door. Claudette was one of these.

Located about a two-hour drive from where I live here in upstate New York is a large casino and resort that is owned and operated by the Oneida Indian Nation. Although I'm not that big of a gambler, I do, occasionally, like to go out and throw the bones; that is, I like to play craps. But I'm not very good at it, and I usually—for lack of a better expression—get scalped.

A greater benefit of visiting this particular casino is that it's an hour's drive (from the opposite direction) to where my father and brothers live, and so every once in a while, we all arrange to meet there for a get-together. First, we enjoy a dinner at the casino's most excellent buffet and catch up on all of the gossip. Then we all go out and try our luck at the crap tables. But even though we mostly lose our money, we still manage to have a good time. One of the problems I had with these outings—that is, *until I learned better*—was I always felt the obligation to phone in to the office to check if I had any messages.

On one particularly beautiful August evening, after meeting at the main entrance to the casino, we went straight to the waiting line for the buffet. As we stood there waiting, I don't know what came over me, but I got the notion to go and call home to check my messages. After dialing the number and punching in my security code to the recorder, I was instantly inundated with a lady's screams and curses about her dying Pekingese with blood all over her white couch and something about not eating for two days. "Poop, poop, poop" [not my exact words] I shouted to myself as I jotted the number down. I dialed back the phone number and said, "Hello Claudette, Dr. Orzeck here, and I'm returning your call. Tell me, please, what's going on with your little dog.

"Oh, Doctor! Thank God you called. Little Tuffy has been bleeding from her private parts for a week, and for the last two days, she hasn't eaten a thing. Now she's just lying there on my couch and can't get up. I'm so afraid she's gonna die. Doctor! You gotta save her!"

Feeling just a touch of disbelief (and a bit of anger rising up within me as well), I simply stood there for a second and assessed the situation. From what I could recall at the time, I knew that Little Tuffy was about a ten-year-old Pekingese mix, whose owner only brought her in to the clinic every once in awhile, just for her rabies shots. Her mother had always refused all other vaccinations, wormings, and the great need to get Little Tuffy's rotten teeth pulled. She'd always responded to my advice in an arrogant and coldly dismissive tone. "Oh, she'll be all right, Doc. And besides," she added as she swept her fifty dollar, blood-red, manicured, bear claw—like fingers over the body of the hapless little dog on the exam table, "I can't afford it."

After a couple more seconds of silence, I spoke. "How long did you say she'd been passing blood?"

She answered that it had been about a week, maybe ten days. As I stood there, I continued to fill with rage, but I resisted—with all of my might—the burning urge to ask her the question I most wanted in the worst way to ask: "Lady, why in the heck did you wait until nine o'clock on a friggin' Saturday night before you decided to call me and completely louse up my weekend?" Instead, I held my tongue and calmly and very professionally asked her a couple more specific questions regarding her Little Tuffy. The question that clinched the diagnosis of the dog's problem was this one: "Claudette, is Tuffy spayed?"

"Ah, no, I don't think so," she answered.

Gently, and with an almost Herculean restraint, I asked her the question again. "Claudette, it's very important, please try to concentrate. How old is Little Tuffy now?"

"About ten years old, Doc."

"And how old was she when you got her?"

"Just about two months old," she replied.

With maybe the slightest hint of sarcastic contempt in my voice, I continued. "Is it at all possible that someone, without your knowledge, could have taken her away and had her spayed?"

"No way," she cried, the indignation apparent in her tone. "She's been with me every day since I've owned her."

And that was that. Without any further questioning, I came to the conclusion that sweet Little Tuffy was not spayed, and, more than likely, the problem she was now suffering from was a severe type of uterine infection known as a pyometra.

For what seemed like minutes—although I'm now sure it was only a couple of seconds—I agonized over what to do next. I knew from experience that pyometras, especially when left untreated for so long, are often fatal. A battle raged back and forth in my head as to what I should do. Should I rush home and do an emergency hysterectomy, or should I just blow it off and enjoy a relaxing evening with my family? My father had recently suffered a heart attack, so seeing him this evening was quite a blessed event.

However, I knew in my heart of hearts that neither Theresa nor I would be able to enjoy the meal; we'd both be too worried about Little Tuffy. From Claudette's description of her little dog's nearly comatose condition, I knew the poisonous toxins that were being released by the bacteria in her pus-filled uterus could probably kill her before the night was over. But then again, it was *Not My Fault* that she'd waited so long before acting; why should my family and I have to suffer because of her procrastination and neglect?

So I quoted her a fairly high estimated price for my services in the hope she'd want to take it somewhere else. "Doctor," she shot back, "she's my baby; money is no object." She added, "And besides, yours has been the cheapest price quote that I've been given."

I was now fuming. All I could think of was: Son of a gun [not my exact words], there she was, on the other end of the phone; her "baby," because of her neglect, was dying before her very eyes, and she's out price shopping. I think that if the conversation went on for much longer, the receiver would have melted in my hand.

Around and around my thoughts went. This way, that way, back and forth, like a Ping-Pong ball, with the final vision ending up being the sight of Little Tuffy lying there dead. Finally, just to end my torment, I said, "OK, Claudette, I'll meet you at the office in exactly two hours. Make sure you're not late."

I could hear the relief in her voice. "OK, Doc, I'll be there."

We both hung up the phone without saying good-bye. As I walked over to the buffet line, I saw that Theresa, my father, and my brothers were now almost to the front. Theresa immediately saw the dejected look on my face as I approached and asked what was wrong.

I filled them all in on the situation. I told them about the owner's waiting till the last minute to call; I told them that if I didn't get this poor little dog into the hospital tonight, by morning it would be too late; and I told them that I'd made an appointment with the owner to meet her in two hours. I hated with all of my heart to say that last statement.

Several quiet moments passed and, by this time, we were all at the head of the line and being requested to enter the restaurant. Without knowing what else to say or do, we just all said good-bye.

My father asked if we could at least stay for the buffet. I answered that it would take too long. I knew and he knew that what I was doing had to be done. He and my family are all loving humanitarians as well as businesspeople; still, I had the aching feeling in my gut that the whole situation just wasn't fair. To this very day, even though over the years we've managed to pull off several of these get-togethers, in my heart of hearts, I'm still not convinced what I did was the right thing. "All right," he said, "you gotta do what you gotta do."

And so we left. We made a quick stop at McDonald's, then got onto the interstate and started the long, quiet ride home.

It was just before midnight when we pulled into the driveway of my clinic; Claudette was waiting for us. I walked through the darkness to the porch, unlocked the door, and turned on the lights. Theresa helped Little Tuffy's owner carry her into the clinic and into my examining room. At first sight, the dog looked like it was dead. Her gums were purple and clammy, her breathing was more like occasional gasps, and her poor little body was ice cold. The telltale, stinking pus that was draining from her backside made the diagnosis of uterine pyometra a sure thing.

Even with as tough a stomach as I have, the fetid smell of the discharge made me gag. My anger, which had calmed some on the car ride home, was again starting to creep back to the surface. Of all of the neglects this owner had shown this little dog, the aspect of the whole situation that made me wonder the most was how in the heck could she have tolerated this awful stench for as long as she did!

After assessing poor Little Tuffy's condition, I gave her owner all of my normal warnings of the possible dangers of anesthesia plus a couple extras. I made it clear to her that her dog's toxic and near-comatose condition, combined with her advanced age, made the surgery I was about to perform extremely risky. I also offered her the option of putting Little Tuffy to sleep in order to avoid the poor creature having to go through the pain of the surgery and long recovery. Claudette answered that she understood the dangers and that there was no way she would ever put the dog down. She then said good-bye, and I admitted Little Tuffy into the hospital.

The first thing I did was attempt to insert an intravenous catheter into her limp little forearm. Because of her toxic condition, the blood pressure to her limbs was quite low, and it took me three tries before I succeeded. After starting the flow of warm, life-giving, fluid into her vein, I laid her on her back and shaved and scrubbed the surgery site. As I did so, I remember thinking to myself about the number of times I've performed surgery for this most preventable of disease.

Pyometra, put in the simplest of terms, is a severe and often life-threatening infection of the uterus in females of all species. Although it can happen at any age and in any breed of dog or cat, I most commonly see it in older, small-breed dogs. In the early stages of the disease, owners often confuse the bloody discharge with a heat cycle. The difference, however, in the case of pyometra, is that the discharge doesn't stop. Over the period of a week or so, the discharge becomes foul-smelling, and the animal starts to become weak and lethargic. If medical care isn't started soon, the toxins released by the festering pus in the animal's uterus will kill her.

Until I realized I was upsetting many owners with this question, I always made it a point to ask why in the world they never had their dog spayed. The most common answers I got were: first, they loved their pet too much to make the poor little thing endure the discomfort of surgery, and second, they simply had never heard of a pyometra. In a personal sort of way, I guess I could see their point.

The next most common answer for not spaying their females was from people who bred their dogs until they got to old to produce anymore pups. Their thinking was that since their dog could no longer get pregnant, there was no longer any need to worry. I guess this makes sense also.

A third group of owners were represented by the it's-just-a-damned-dog bunch who never felt any need whatsoever to get their females—or males— fixed. (It's best not to ask me what most of these people do with all of their unwanted pups and kittens.)

The last group of owners who choose not to spay their pets are what some people might consider just a little bit strange. They choose not to alter their pets because of some notion of disturbing their pet's intrinsic femaleness, whatever that means. These people, however, often change their mind fairly quickly, usually just after their little vixen's first heat has every unneutered male dog from within a five-mile radius hanging out around their home. If all of those studs hanging around their yards having urinating contests and dogfights doesn't induce them to spay their little darlings, then they'll definitely get the surgery done after an unexpected mating occurs and the dog's femaleness blesses them with about fourteen screaming little mixed breed puppies.

After scrubbing and gloving up, I started Little Tuffy's surgery. In a routine spay, I would have normally made about a two-inch-long incision, entered the abdominal cavity, and removed two kidney bean—sized ovaries and a uterus about the size of two pencils. For Little Tuffy's surgery, I was going to have to make about a six-inch-long cut, being extremely careful as I did so not to accidentally slice into the super-sized, pus-filled, fragile uterus.

When I'd gotten into her abdomen, I could see that her uterus was the size of two men's socks filled to near the rupturing point. I stood there for a second analyzing the situation and trying to get my courage up. I then gently stuck my finger deep into her abdomen and, hooking it around the body of the uterus, I lifted it up through the opening. By the time I had the entire uterus out of her belly, it looked like two big throbbing pepperoni sticks joined at one end.

I then proceeded to tie off and remove each ovary, and then I did the same at the uterus's base, just above the cervix. I clamped and cut all of its body attachments, lifted it off her belly, and then dropped it into a waiting two-gallon bucket my wife keeps in our clinic for just such emergencies. I sewed Little Tuffy back up, gave her some antibiotics, disconnected her fluids, and took her home to my house so Theresa and I could keep an eye on her. Because she hadn't moved a single bit since her owner carried her into the office, I was convinced she was not going to live out the night.

But I was wrong. About four A.M., she started to rouse some, and so Theresa woke up and got her to drink some water. The following morning, we took her back to the clinic, hooked her back up to the intravenous fluids, and gave her enough to get her kidneys working again. Later on, she even managed to walk around outside and urinate on her own. We called her mother and offered to let her come in during the office hours to visit. She said that she had a date that night and couldn't come in. I was a little perplexed and could feel a touch of the anger rising up from my innards. I asked, "Claudette, what about all of this 'she's my baby, Doc' crap you gave me last night?

"Oh, she'll be fine, Doc. I'll come see her tomorrow." And she hung up the phone. And that was that.

Little Tuffy was ready the next day to go home. She was eating some and was peeing up a storm. When her mother came in that night, and while Theresa went into the cage room to get Little Tuffy, I handed Claudette her bill. She looked at it, and then, like it was the most natural thing in the world to do, she said, "I'll stop in this weekend to pay ya."

I was floored. With a stare I'm sure would have turned a rattlesnake's head away, I said, "Hold on there, Claudette, you said money was no object! I left my family alone in a restaurant, drove like a madman for two hours, operated on your little dog until two in the morning, and now you're telling me you're not gonna pay me!"

"Oh, I will, as soon as I get the money," she assured me.

Theresa, who was standing in the doorway to the kennel room, asked me what I wanted to do. I told her I wasn't quite sure. The law says I could keep the dog in the hospital until she paid her bill. And if the truth were to be told, I actually thought about doing just that because I had the worst feeling, which ultimately turned out to be true, that this young lady was going to stiff me with the bill.

But I decided against it. Little Tuffy was very nervous about being in the hospital, and I was afraid her being in this anxious state would affect her recovery. So I took a chance and decided to send her home. I couldn't take it anymore.

And so I told my wife, "Give her the darn [not the exact word I used] dog." Then, turning around to Little Tuffy's owner, in as a controlled and stern a voice as I could muster, I said, "Claudette, I want to be paid!"

She grabbed her dog from my wife's arms, and as snooty and as viciously as she possibly could, snarled, "Doc, you go to hell! I'll pay you if I feel like it," and she slammed the front door behind her.

Postscript

I sort of took the whole thing of Claudette not paying her bill quite personally. I knew from speaking with friends of hers that she wasn't in any way destitute or else I'd have let the whole thing slide and chalk it to another learning experience. But she had a very good-paying job as a dental receptionist, and because of some mental defect, she just choose not to pay her bills.

So for the next six months, my wife or I would call her (it was mostly my wife because every time I spoke with the woman, I'd be cranky for two days), and politely and very professionally request payment for saving her dog's life. And we would have continued doing so, except that she moved to a neighboring town and got an unlisted number. It turns out she owed everyone money. Finally, in desperation, I hired a private collection agent.

Apparently this collection lady must have used some fairly strong tactics, because I started getting calls from Claudette asking me to please call this women off of her case. I told Claudette that as soon as she paid up, I would be happy to do so.

It got so bad for her, that a week later, Claudette phoned and threatened me by saying she was going to call the state attorney general and report me. I told her to go ahead; I didn't care. She was calling me, I wasn't calling her.

In a mild sort of way, I was actually beginning to enjoy the whole drama.

I was told several weeks later by an old boyfriend of hers that she did indeed call the attorney general. But whoever answered the phone at the state office told Claudette her complaints had no merit; she was firmly told to just pay her bills like she should.

After several more weeks of silence, she called me up at the office and pleaded with me to call off the bill collector. She then promised me that as soon as her income tax refund came in, she'd pay me in full. I said to her that her word of honor meant nothing anymore to me, and that I was getting tired of hearing her whine. I told her the whole thing was in the hands of the bill collector, and she'd have to take it up with her. And I never heard from her again.

About a month later, I received a check in the mail from the collection agent for the full amount of Little Tuffy's bill.

Chapter Twelve

Dominion Over the Beasts

The following is a true story. The details have been changed just a tiny bit in order to protect the innocent.

It was just about closing time during weekday office hours when an emergency phone call came in to the office. On the other end of the line was the daughter of an elderly couple whose old dog, Luke, I'd seen (thankfully) only a few times before. She seemed quite calm, maybe even a little cheerful, considering the serious nature of the dog's emergency.

"Doc, my parents wanted me to call you in advance and warn ya that they're bringing in Ol' Luke. They wanted me to tell ya he's been shot up pretty bad."

The daughter went on to say that Ol' Luke had been out running again and sowing his wild oats, and somebody went and shot him.

As she spoke, I thought to myself it was more likely the old boy was out chasing deer or harassing some farmer's livestock, and a game warden or some other concerned citizen blasted him with a shotgun.

"How bad is he?" I asked.

"I'm not sure, Doc, I didn't see him. I guess he somehow or another managed to drag himself back home to the ditch next to the road in front of the house, but Ma did tell me that his guts are hangin' out his side."

Oh boy, I thought to myself as I pondered the possibilities, *this sounds like its going to be a real mess.* I told the daughter I'd wait around, thanked her for the warning, and hung up.

And so I stuck around past closing time, and sure enough, about ten minutes later, Ol' Luke and his mommy and his daddy pulled into the clinic's driveway in their old Dodge pickup. I grabbed my plywood stretcher and helped them carry the dog into the exam room. As I pulled the blanket he'd been wrapped in away from his body, I could tell instantly he'd been shot broadside in the chest and abdomen by a shotgun.

Ol' Luke was an enormous and intact (which is a polite way of saying he still had his coconuts), black Labrador retriever. During the six years I had him as a patient, I didn't see a whole lot of Ol' Luke because his parents only brought him into the office every couple of years just to get his required rabies vaccinations. And that was fine with me for two reasons.

First of all, he was not all that well behaved. His parents had no control over him whatsoever. Every time they brought him to my clinic, he would bark and growl and try to attack any other unfortunate animal that happened to be in the waiting room. I was forever thankful that his daddy used an old chunk of log chain for Ol' Luke's collar and leash. Also, despite every effort of my wife or me to prevent him from doing so, I can't recall a single visit in which the nasty beast didn't end up hiking his leg and peeing about a half dozen times on the walls of my waiting room.

But an even bigger reason I was glad to not to see him all that often was because, ever since the very first day he laid eyes on me, Ol' Luke just plain outright hated my guts. I'm serious; he wanted to kill me. He was so ferocious that the act of giving him a simple rabies shot was a death defying ordeal for me. As a matter of fact, the dog was so ornery that even as he lay there in my exam room with a hundred shotgun pellets in his body, in shock and unable to lift his head or move his back legs, and with a good portion of his entrails pouring out of a hole in his belly and festooning down the side of the exam table, the cranky old son of a gun still managed to muster up a snarl and take a vicious snap at me.

After a quick exam, I told Ol' Luke's mommy and daddy that his chances of surviving weren't too good; from what I could tell by just looking through the gaping hole in his flank, most of his abdominal organs were perforated and torn to shreds by the shotgun pellets. Likewise, because of his gurgling breathing, I was sure he was bleeding into his chest cavity.

The biggest question in my mind, however, was the condition of his spinal cord. He couldn't move either of his hind legs, and when I pinched his hind toes hard with a large pair of forceps, there was no reaction at all. My worst fear, therefore, was that Ol' Luke might be permanently paralyzed.

I very gently told his parents that before we got too carried away with trying to save Ol' Luke, I should do an X ray and see if there were any shotgun pellets in his spinal cord or heart. I explained to them that because of Ol' Luke's "charming" personality, there was no way in the world I'd be able to move him around on an X ray table while he was still awake; therefore, I'd have to sedate him first. And, because of his serious condition, there would be a substantial risk of death as a result of using the anesthetic, and he might not wake up.

I also gave them the option of not making the poor dog endure any of these lifesaving efforts at all and just put him humanely out of his misery.

After giving his owners all of these warnings and then reminding them one last time that Ol' Luke's chances for surviving his injuries were slim to none, I waited for their response.

After a couple of seconds of considerate and loving thought, the husband looked over at his wife, and she looked back at him. Then they both looked down at Ol' Luke lying there on the exam room table. The old boy's chest rose and fell violently as he gasped for each breath. He literally was holding on to life by a thread. After a couple more seconds of silent deliberation, they looked back up at each other and nodded their heads in silent agreement. Then they both looked over at me.

"Doc," said the wife, "I think we'd both feel better if you gave it a try. We know he ain't the best behaved dog in the world, but he's a good dog, and he's always been a good friend. We'd like you to do what you can to help him."

I have to admit I was a little surprised by this answer. I could only wonder what in the world they could have been thinking. In my mind, the situation looked so obviously hopeless, I felt certain they would have chosen the option of putting him down. However, it was not my place to question their decision. If they wanted to try to save him, I'd give it my best.

And so, with the tone in my voice of the guy who was going to have the job of putting poor old Humpty Dumpty back together again, I said, "OK, folks, I'll do the best I can," and I began preparing the injection of anesthetic.

But as I did so, I could see by the concerned look on the face of the wife as she stood there, watching her beloved pet, that something else was troubling her. I saw her then look back over toward her husband as if she wanted him to say something. When he didn't, she looked back over toward her dying old friend. After a second or two had passed, she reached down and gently picked up his front paw and looked at it. And looked at it. And looked at it some more.

Greatly touched by her tenderness at this most difficult of times, my first thought was that she was just holding his hand in a sincere and motherly gesture of farewell, and that any moment she would break down in an unbridled expression of grief. But I was wrong.

"Doctor," she said, as she lovingly placed Ol' Luke's paw back down on the table and looked back up toward me, "do you think that while he's under, you could clip his nails for us?"

"Huh?" I asked, a little bit stunned by her request. I mean, here we were, the poor critter was minutes away from death, and all she could think about was making sure his nails were trimmed. Although I kept my thoughts to myself, I'm sure the look utter disbelief on my face gave me away.

Before I had a chance to say another word, she pleaded, "Doctor, he just fights us to no end when we try to clip his nails. The last time we tried, he bit my husband on the ear. I don't know why he don't like it. I figured that as long as he was out, it would be a good time to do it."

One more time, all I could do was just stand there in wonder at this bizarre request. "OK," I said as I gathered up Ol' Luke's intestines onto a sterile drape sheet and began carrying him off to the X ray room.

"Thank you, Doctor," said the wife. "We sure do appreciate what you're doing."

To make a long story short, the xrays showed us that several of the shotgun pellets had embedded themselves in Ol' Luke's spinal cord. With this clear evidence that their dog would probably never walk again, his parents decided it would be best to put him down. I then gave Ol' Luke his injection of euthanasia solution, replaced his guts back inside his belly, and sewed all of the holes shut so they wouldn't come flopping back out. I wrapped him up in a blanket (yes, I trimmed his nails) and carried him out to his parents' pickup. They thanked me for all my efforts and took the old boy home and buried him in their apple orchard.

With the possible exceptions of traversing a live minefield, walking down a narrow jungle trail infested with king cobras, or, even worse, giving a worm pill to a cat, I don't think there's any aspect of pet care that raises the level of terror in the hearts of an owner as much as having to trim their dog's toenails. I think some owners would rather endure a root canal—without anesthesia!

And I guess if I was really pressed on the issue, I'd have to admit that I ain't none too crazy about doing it, either. Now, before I get myself into too much trouble, I need to make it perfectly clear that I *do* have patients who are amazingly well behaved when it comes to getting their toenails trimmed, and they are an absolute joy; they'll lie on their sides or stand like little angels as I give them their pedicure and never once wince or complain. But these good guys are few and far between.

My reasons for not relishing the joys of doing toenail trims are many. First, and probably the worst, is that most dogs just plain don't like it. They have to be restrained (which most dogs absolutely hate), and it's very likely that the physical act of actually cutting the nails may cause them some discomfort.

Secondly, it has been my experience that if there's going to be any strain on my doctor/client relationship, it will most likely occur during the process of trimming the nails of an unwilling pet. Not too often, but enough to where it really bothers me, an owner—who conveniently forgets the fact that they themselves are utterly helpless when it comes to performing this most simple of tasks—is somehow angered with me by the need to have them, any spouse or siblings they may have brought along with them, me, my wife, and/or any willing volunteers who might be in the waiting room hold down and restrain their little killer Pekingese in order to trim the beast's toenails. I've had people walk out and never return because they didn't like the way I did their "sweet" little Precious's toenails. They think I'm purposely hurting their little baby.

But the biggest reason I'm not crazy about doing nails is the frequent pain and suffering it often causes. And I'm talking about *my* pain and suffering here. When I look back at the times I've been seriously bitten, nearly blinded as a dog's needle-pointed claw raked across my face, or have been nearly knocked unconscious by a struggling rottweiler's thick skull rapping up against my forehead, it would have to be while I was trimming a dog's toenails. Likewise, I don't think a single day goes by in which Theresa or I don't have to mop up after a dog who's emptied its bladder or forcefully evacuated its rectum— i.e., squirted crap all over the table, walls, and floor—while being held down for a nail clipping.

But as bad as I make it sound, just like going to the dentist, getting your prostate checked if you're over fifty years old, or paying income taxes, trimming dogs' toenails is one of those things you have to do if you're a veterinarian, and I try to always try to put on a happy face. Like the sneaker commercial always says: "Just do it!" And I do.

I have this recurring dream.

After I've passed on from this earthly existence, and our Lord finds me acceptable to enter his Heavenly Kingdom, I'm standing at the Pearly Gates. All wise and loving Saint Peter opens the gate and lets me in. "Come on in, Doc, it's good to finally see ya."

But as I pass through the gate and start walking away into the Realm of Eternity, the blessed saint stops me and says, "Hey Doc, I hate to bother you, but I got this big Saint Bernard He's a great dog, Doc, just as gentle as a lamb. All of the little angels and cherubs just love him. But he's got one terrible problem: he hates to have his nails trimmed. Doc, as long as you're in the area, would you mind . . ."

Chapter Thirteen

Wonders Everywhere

One of the pleasures I miss from the early years of my veterinary career is making farm visits and small animal house calls. Oh, I still make an occasional call; however, they're usually limited to visiting households with a large number of pets in need of vaccinations or an at-home euthanasia if the owner is unable to bring a pet in. I also do an occasional farm call for a neighbor who might need my help delivering a calf or lamb.

The reasons I stopped doing farm calls are many, but the main one was because of economics. In the area where we live, the family dairy farm is an endangered species. There just aren't that many in business anymore, and I personally feel great sadness at their passing. When I did get a call out to a farm, I'd have to put on my coveralls and boots, drive anywhere from five to twenty-five miles one way, spend an hour or two pregnancy checking cows, treating a couple of cases of mastitis (mammary gland infections), or trim a few hooves. After I was finished, I'd have to listen to the farmer for ten minutes complaining about my bill, and then drive back home to take a shower.

This was not a problem at first, because I didn't have that many dog and cat clients. However, as the small animal aspect of my practice grew, I found myself more and more pressed for time. Once in a while, I'd get tied up at a farm and would not have time to clean up or even change my clothes before my office hours were scheduled to begin. To put it bluntly, sometimes I smelled like cow poop. Sadly, or maybe not so sadly, considering the antiseptic day in which we now live, I got more than one offended look and even a couple of disapproving comments.

I brushed these negative reactions off by telling the client a story from my own childhood in which I, too, was guilty of this very same sin. I remember my family and I, while driving down a country road, once passed a snow-covered cornfield on which a dairy farmer had just finished spreading manure. The contrast of the splattered brown manure on top of the shiny white snow was something I hadn't seen before, and when I was told by my father what it was, I remember holding my nose and commenting on how bad it smelled. My dear grandmother, who was sitting in the backseat with my brothers and me, firmly but in her gentle way told me, "Grandson, that's the smell of money!"

She had been born and raised on a dairy farm, and she spent the next ten minutes explaining to me the subject of good dairy cow health: how a cow needs to eat lots of hay and grain in order to make lots of milk, and that the more the cow eats, the more it has to poop. She went on explaining how hard farmers had to work, getting up early to milk the cows, working all day in the fields, and then, when evening came, they still had to go out and milk the cows all over again. But even when I told this story to offended clients, I could tell by the their glassy stares and constricted nostrils that they still didn't appreciate my smelling like a cow barn while examining their little doggie.

I thought it was a little sad, but that's the way it is, and I guess it's always been like that since the dawn of civilization. Whether society likes to admit it or not, there is an unquestionable difference between the people of the cities, suburbs, and villages of this world, and those who live on the farm. The metropolitan dwellers always have—and probably always will—continue to live off the fruits of farmers' sweat and blood, and that's OK. But God forbid any of them should have to endure a whiff of cow manure now and then.

Anyway, as time went on, I found it no longer possible to continue both aspects of my practice. With a heavy heart, I first stopped doing farm calls. Then about a year later, I cut back on all but the gravest of emergencies in small animal house calls.

But I do miss getting out on those calls. I miss most the long rides through the country and watching the procession of the seasons: the spring with farmers plowing and planting their corn and wheat. Then as the spring slips into summer, there would be the overwhelming green in the forests, the hayfields, and the vineyards. With autumn would come the harvests, the radiance of the fall foliage, and the crisp, breathlessly clear, star-filled nights. The winter, with the countryside calm and peaceful under a blanket of snow, however, could be a pain in the neck.

One of the more memorable and wondrous farm calls of my veterinary career happened in the autumn following my graduation from vet school. I was still working for my first boss and was on the weekend shift by myself. A dairy farmer, from a farm located quite far from the practice, called and said he had a downed cow out in his pasture who'd just had a baby, and he wanted me to come out as soon as possible. I told him I had a few other emergencies to contend with, but that I'd try my darnedest to get out to his farm before dark. He said OK, and after I asked him for the directions to his farm, we hung up.

As fate would have it, I never got there till about seven o'clock, and it was as dark a moonless night as could be imagined. But the farmer was in good spirits, and he had the situation well in hand. With the help of his two sons, a four-by-four pickup, a lantern, and several flashlights, we set out driving up this huge hill behind his barn that served as his cow pasture. Up and up we went until we came to the end of the trail. As the two boys grabbed my medical bag and two buckets of warm water from the bed of the pickup, the oldest said, "Doc, we're gonna have to walk from here on. The cow ain't too far up though; only about a quarter of a mile."

It was one of the longest and hardest quarter miles I'd ever had to climb! Even though the farmer and his sons graciously carried everything we needed, including my medical bag, I still found the climb a struggle. I guess it was because I'd been at this cow-saving stuff since five A.M. that morning, and I was just plain pooped. But when I look back on that night, it was all worth it.

As we topped the hill and I walked over to where the cow was lying on her side, her newborn calf standing timid and hungry beside her, one of the most magnificent panoramas I'd ever seen was unfolding in the valley below. It turned out to be a U.S. Air Force base, completely turned on and lit up as far as my eye could see in order to guide in a squadron of B-52 bombers which, as I stood there in awe, were coming in just over our heads. I couldn't contain myself. "Holy cow; this is amazing!" I exclaimed over and over. I was so transfixed that the farmer, who was a little worried about his cow, had to snap me out of it.

"I know, Doc," the father said. "I never cease to be amazed at it myself. It's a pretty incredible sight, but now we got to save this cow." Back into the reality of the situation, I then knelt down next to the cow and began my examination. After checking her out from head to toe, I concluded she probably had a bad case of milk fever. No problem. Even though it's called milk fever, there's usually no fever; the disease is an acute calcium deficiency that responds marvelously to intravenous calcium-loaded fluids.

We got the cow's head raised up enough for me to get an IV line started in the jugular vein of her neck. I attached a bottle of calcium and, while the youngest son held it in the air, I let the life-giving fluid slowly drip into her vein. When the first bottle was empty, I attached a second one. Before this second bottle was even halfway finished, the cow started struggling, wanting to get up. I quickly pulled the IV needle from her vein just as she rose to her feet.

After a couple of minutes of unsteadiness, she and her baby, followed by the youngest son, all started walking down the mountain back to the barn. The farmer, the oldest son, and I stayed behind for a few minutes. We casually talked about all of the things farmers everywhere talk about: the price of milk, the weather, the success of some crops and the failure of others, all the while watching the action in the valley below.

But after several minutes, even though I was enjoying the show, I started getting a little anxious to begin heading back down; I still had one more emergency to attend to. But the farmer said, "Hey Doc, let's just hold on a second. They're almost done landing the planes. You gotta see what happens next." And no sooner had the words come out of his mouth than, from east to west and north to south, the lights all went out. It was like somebody pulled a gigantic master light switch. All you could see were a few scattered lighted buildings and hangars. And the stars! Unbelievable!

The farm calls I used to make to treat dairy cows were my favorite. But I have to admit that I also enjoyed making house calls to treat cats and dogs. One of the greatest pleasures of doing these calls to people's homes was that it gave me a chance to really get to know my clients, see what books they read, and learn of any hobbies or special interests they might have. It's my feeling that as we go through our lives, we tend to associate with people as nearly like ourselves as possible. We don't see the entire spectrum of all that exists out there in our world with regards to the talents, personalities, and lifestyles of our fellow human beings. I find this, also, a little sad.

In the area where I did most of my small animal house calls, we had a lot of artists, both professional and amateur. Being somewhat of an armchair art lover (as well as a closet abstract art painter), I always found these visits especially fascinating. One time, I was called to an elderly lady's home to give shots and trim the toenails of her Siamese cat. Nearly every wall of her house was covered with magnificent watercolor paintings she'd done of every type of flower you could imagine; it was like stepping into the Garden of Eden. After finishing treating her cat (trimming the toenails of the little guy drew blood from both her son and me), we talked for a long time about art, and painting, and flowers. She was quite a lady, and I was thrilled when she offered me my choice of any one of her paintings as payment for my services.

One of the most unusual house calls I made (with regards to art) was to a fellow who, because of severe arthritis in his hips, spent most of his time shut in his house. When he made the appointment over the phone, he said he just had a little Lhasa apso who needed his vaccinations and, as always is the case, the dog's bearclaw—like toenails had to be trimmed. I arrived at his house the next day, and after sweeping the snow from my boots (it was the dead of winter) on his front porch landing, I stepped through the front door into his living room.

Without the slightest bit of warning, I was suddenly surrounded by hundreds of the weirdest but at the same time most dazzling oil paintings I've ever seen. They were on every square inch of every wall; huge canvases depicting—and I'm afraid that my attempt to describe these works of art is hopelessly inadequate—agonizing visions of a world that no man should ever have to see; however, there was also a beauty, a calmness, a release of spirit that was overpowering. There were swirls of living color, gobbed on rather than painted; the forms were animal-like but not of this universe. I found them quite exciting. We talked a long time about art, his suffering, and how his painting makes it all bearable. I, again, was thrilled when he offered me my choice of any painting as payment for my vet services.

But many house calls I made weren't quite so enlightening. Sometimes the darker underbelly of our society reared its ugly head. When it did, it was never a pretty sight. One early autumn afternoon, as a courtesy to one of my local county health departments, I did a house call to a home that was supposed to have about twenty-five cats. I was to be met at the client's house by a social worker.

The social worker, who was one of the most dedicated, selfless, and loving persons I've ever met—plus she was also a super animal lover herself—had arranged this call strictly on her own initiative. Her client, a mildly retarded woman, had somehow managed to accumulate a large number of cats, none of which had ever had any vaccinations. The social worker, among many other things, was worried about the possibility of her client or one of the client's year-old little girls getting exposed to rabies from a bite from one of these cats. She negotiated a special price for my service, helped her client save up enough money (I'm sure that my friend ended up paying for a good part of it herself), and the day before I made the call, she helped round up the cats.

As we talked about how were going to tackle this big project, her client came walking out of the house. She was a big woman, young, maybe about twenty-five years old. She was wearing a large orange muumuu-type dress and was barefoot. A cigarette dangled from the left side of her mouth. Without any greeting of hello or anything, she pointed to a small shed in her backyard and said, "We got most of them in there." I grabbed several needles and syringes and a couple of vials of vaccine, and the two of us followed her into the yard.

Vaccinating these wild little beasts turned into a life-or-death ordeal. Although the client knew them all by name and could handle most of them, the cats were not used to seeing anyone else, and every last one of them fought us like little tigers. The lady, without the slightest fear, would bend down, stick her arm through the slightly opened door of the shed, and just grab one of the savage little creatures anywhere she could. (About every third time she bent over, one or both of her gigantic breasts would flop out over the top of her muumuu—to my embarrassment—and she'd have to stand up, and like it was the most natural thing in the world to do, stuff them back in.)

Then, while she and the social worker did their best to restrain each flailing and thrashing cat, I'd inject it anywhere I could with rabies vaccine. After about two hours, all three of us, bloody but unbowed, were done. All that had to be done now was fill out the rabies certificates. The cat owner suggested we go into her house to do the paperwork.

As I look back on this adventure, it would have been an amusing experience, a funny story I could tell my classmates at reunion, had I not gone into this poor woman's home. As we all walked across the front porch and through the front door into the living room, the first thing that happened was I was nearly knocked out by the smell. I don't want to sound condescending or snobbish about this—I've been in chicken barns, I've been swatted in the face by rotten, maggot-infested cow afterbirths, and have stood up to my knees in pig poop—but this house reeked. It was a combination of vomit, beer, and human feces, with a little bit of tomcat urine thrown in. Sitting on a grimy sofa was an older man, the client's boyfriend at the time, watching The Weather Channel on this immense, big-screen TV. But what upset me most was that in the middle of the living room, crawling around in their diapers on the filthy carpet, were two of the most adorable little children you would ever want to see. One, obviously, needed her diapers changed.

After clearing off a spot on the coffee table, I began to fill out the rabies forms. But I couldn't concentrate; all I could do was worry about the two little girls. The social worker, seeing the one child needed to be changed, asked her client where the Pampers were. This question about the Pampers suddenly brought the man sitting on the sofa to life.

Out of the blue, even though it wasn't his money (the woman was on public assistance), the man started complaining about how much it was costing them to buy food and diapers for the babies. A little upset by his remarks, I forced a smile and asked him how much his cable TV bill was. He then started complaining about how the rate had gone so high that he might have to cancel The Playboy Channel because he couldn't any longer afford it. I then asked him what he did for a living. He said he couldn't work because he had a bad back. I wanted to ask him how much they paid for the big-screen TV but decided against it. It would have just pissed me off even more.

After I finished the paperwork, and just before the social worker and I were walked out the front door, I turned around, took one more look at those two little babies, and my heart just broke. As I walked across the front lawn to my car, I again turned around and stopped; I wanted in the worst way to run back into the house, pick those two little girls up, and take them away from that misery. But the social worker, almost as if she was reading my mind, said to me, "Doc, forget it. There is nothing that can be done. Soon, the county will very likely put them in a foster home, just like they did with her previous six children." I asked her how something like this could happen. She said she didn't know but assured me she would make sure it turned out OK for the kids. We then thanked each other for the experience and I got in my car and drove away. Although I've seen the social worker a hundred times since, I never had the nerve to ask her about the two little girls; I just don't want to know.

If someone was to ask me which was the most bizarre or most totally unexpected house call I'd ever been out on, it would have to be the time I was called out by a client to look at a dying goat. The call would combine eccentricity, revulsion, wonder, just a hint of danger, and even a pleasant bonus thrown in for good measure.

I should have expected something unusual was going to happen when the daughter of the goat owner called from a pay phone. When you're the owner of a business, a pay phone call nearly always alerts you to one of two important facts: either the person calling can't afford a phone, or they live so far off the beaten path that phone service is not available. In the case of this house call, both turned out to be true. After filling me in on what she thought the problem with the goat was, she gave me directions to her mother's house trailer and hung up.

It was nearly dark out before I could get out on the call. I had recalled seeing this home a few times in my travels, so I had no trouble finding it. The home was a fairly new house trailer that sat about a quarter of a mile from the road in the middle of an old, overgrown cornfield. Surrounding the house and filling up every square inch of the front yard were about a million wooden shipping pallets stacked up as far as a man could reach.

I remember wondering as I pulled into the muddy driveway how in the world they were ever going to get electricity way the heck out there in the middle of this field; the nearest electric pole was about three miles back toward town. After a second of pondering this question, I made the assumption that these were probably going to be just simple homesteaders who wanted to get away from it all. I remember thinking, "More power to them."

But this would not be the case. After getting out of my vetmobile, I grabbed my medical bag from the back and started walking to the front door. As I climbed the pile of pallets that served as both their front porch and stairs, I noticed a tiny, very old man who, with a rusty handsaw, was sawing up one of the pallets for what I assumed was going to be fire-wood. I chuckled to myself as I remembered the early, lean days of my marriage, doing the very same thing (only I had a chain saw). The man never looked up or said a word, even after I said hello; he just kept on sawing up that pallet.

I knocked on the front door. From inside I could hear a great commotion, and then silence. After a couple seconds of this silence, there was a scream, "Come on in!" I hesitated for a second—it all seemed a little creepy—but then pushed in on the door and took a step inside. The hallway was dark, and as I made this first step into the trailer, I immediately lost my balance and fell forward, slamming into the wall across from the door. The trailer, to my great surprise, had not been leveled out yet, and the floor sloped downhill side to side at quite a sharp angle.

After regaining my balance, the next sensation to hit me was the strong smell of urine, woodsmoke, and the kerosene fumes coming from the two Coleman lanterns that lighted up the living room. But then, as my eyes adjusted to the light, I saw the most amazing thing. Stacked from wall to ceiling were cage after cage of exotic birds of every kind: parrots, cockatoos, canaries, parakeets, cockatiels. The first thought I had was that there must be about ten thousand dollars' worth of birds here.

But before I could give them any more thought, a lady's voice howled out from somewhere down a dark hall, "We're back here; she's not doin' too well." Feeling like I was back at sea during a typhoon, I braced myself with my elbow against the downhill wall as I walked through the dark toward the voice.

There, in what was at one time a back bedroom were two young goats, an older lady (who was doing all of the hollering), and a middle-aged man (probably her son) who just stood there holding a lantern. After introducing myself, I started asking her what she thought was wrong with her goats. She told me that she just couldn't get either of them to put on any weight, and one was so weak now, she could no longer stand up.

I asked her when was the last time they'd been wormed, and she answered, "I can't afford the worm pills." I asked her if she fed them any grain or mineral supplements, and she told me flat out, "They don't need to eat anything else, they got good hay." I found myself becoming just a touch irritated by her snotty tone, but I held my tongue and did my best to maintain a professional demeanor. And so, as calmly as I could, I asked her if I could look at some of the hay to see how just how good it was. Without a thought, she yelled to the man holding the lantern to get a slab of hay to show me.

A second later he returned with a moldy, rotten handful of the worst-looking hay you could ever imagine. After closely examining the sample, I asked her if this is what the goats had been getting fed all along. She quickly snapped back that it was. She added, "And I don't want you to tell me this hay ain't no good. The last vet I had out here told me that, and I run her off the property."

Hmm, I thought to myself, *Richard, there's nothing you can tell this lady that she doesn't already know. No matter what you say, she's going to find fault, so just tell her the truth.* And so I did. I told her that this (as I held up the rotten slab of hay) was her problem: this crap she was forcing these poor little goats to eat had no nutrition value at all. I told her that even though their little bellies might be full, they weren't getting any goodness from the food because it was pure crap; she was literally starving the poor creatures to death. For dramatic effect, I held the slab of hay about a foot in front of her face and told her—in no uncertain terms—that I wouldn't use this stuff for bedding in a pigpen.

When I mentioned this last comment to the lady, she had a cow! I mean, she was furious! She began ranting, "I've been raising animals for years. You damned vets don't know poop [not her exact words]. How dare you tell me I'm starving my animals." And on and on she raved for about two minutes. I decided, at that moment, I'd better start making my way back to the door, just in case she wanted to become violent.

As I backed slowly out of the room and down the tilted hallway, I politely told her, "Ma'am, I don't care a hoot what you think. You are starving those poor little creatures to death, whether you like to admit it or not. They need to be wormed, and they need to be fed grain and minerals." And then I shut up. Although I wanted to really tell her all of what I was thinking, I could feel the anger rising from deep within me; and from past experience, I knew I'd better hold my tongue before I said something I shouldn't.

The lady just stood there staring at me until I finished. She looked like a mad dog ready to pounce at my throat. But I stood my ground, and after a couple of seconds, I could see her starting to calm down. Probably expecting some sympathy from me, she said, "Doctor, it's not my fault. We just moved here, and I can't afford to feed them guys like I should."

Poop, poop, poop, I thought to myself [again, poop wasn't the exact word I used] as I stood there trying to figure out what to do. After having driven all the way out here to this person's house, after having to witness the willful neglect of these two poor, starving creatures, and worst of all, after having to listen to the ignorant babble from this disturbed woman, I came to the realization that there was a pretty fair chance I wasn't going to be compensated for my time.

And so, without slightest amount of misgiving, realizing that I had nothing to lose, I went on the offensive. Pointing to the stacks and stacks of birds, I said, "Ma'am, you've got thousands of dollars' worth of birds here. Why didn't you sell a couple of them to help pay your feed bill?"

Making this suggestion was a big mistake. She proceeded to have another cow: "You can't tell me what to do! Who the heck [again, not the exact word she used] do you think you are? Those birds are my whole life. They're my babies, my children. I've hand-raised every one of them. Nobody's going to tell me what to do with my animals." And on and on . . . till finally, she pointed to the front door and howled, "Get out of my house!"

As I stood my ground trying to figure out what to do next, and even though I knew what the answer was going to be, I mentioned to her the delicate subject of paying my bill for this house call. This ticked her off even worse: "How dare you have the nerve to charge me! You didn't do a thing. You don't know what you're talking about. I've been raising animals for years. You're full of poop!" [Again, poop was not the exact word she used.] And on and on again.

After a couple of minutes of listening to her babbling and coming to the final conclusion that there was still no way I was ever going to be paid for this call, I came upon a plan.

I reached down and picked up a cage that had three happy little canaries in it. I then looked her straight in the eye and politely said, "Ma'am, I'm going to take this cage of birds as collateral on your bill. If you or your daughter don't stop into my office by this time next week, I'm keeping them." And I started walking toward the door. As I did, I could see the son coming from the back room holding a steak knife in his hands. At the same time, the old man, who I'd earlier seen sawing up a pallet in the front yard, came walking through the front door with a small hatchet.

A little bit nervous but not in the least afraid (I was pretty mad about the whole situation), I reached down with my right hand and grabbed a piece of sawed-up two-by-four from their pile of firewood that had a large sixteen-penny nail sticking out of the end of it. I held it up, and as I stepped toward the door, I yelled, "OK guys, the first one of you bums [bums was not the exact word I used] that comes near me gets this between his eyes." Both backed away without a word. Even Ma, who'd been a raging bull just seconds before, stood there, mouth open and dumb.

As I slowly eased my way down the stack of pallets toward my vetmobile, I reminded them all one more time that I'd hold the birds for one week. From her front door, the lady started spewing forth a torrent of obscenities, threats about calling the police, and lots of nasty things about my mother. I could still hear her ranting as I backed out of her driveway and headed home. I never saw her or her family again (word has it their trailer was condemned by the county health department), all of which made my wife happy, because she just adored those birds I brought home.

Chapter Fourteen

All Kinds of Owners

One of the most important tools we veterinarians often use when we are trying to diagnose a disease in a pet is the owner's observations and perceptions. This is because most animals, when they come into a vet's office, never ever (it seems) show signs of their problem.

The same thing happens a lot of the time to us. For example, you go to the family physician for a bad cough that's been gnawing at your throat for days; you sit there waiting on a cold exam table, on a slippery sheet of white paper, feeling all the while like a little puppy who's being potty trained; and then, as soon as the doctor comes into the exam room, the cough miraculously disappears. Likewise, the same thing happens when you take your automobile to the car repair shop. For reasons known only to God, that flashing Check Engine light on the dashboard, which has been driving you crazy for two days, suddenly no longer lights up.

So it is with us veterinarians. We must depend on the owner's awareness of changes in their pet's actions and behaviors more than any other diagnostic procedure we could perform. And over the years, I've seen a huge range of pet owners' individual awareness. There is everything from the overly enthusiastic, "weigh, measure, and record the amount of each bowel movement" type (yes, many dog owners actually do this), to the completely unconscious "Doc, it's just a damned dog" type.

One of the best examples of the extremely vigilant owner that stands out in my mind is a sweet, elderly lady who I'll refer to as Mrs. T. During one of her frequent visits to my clinic, as soon as she entered my exam room, she immediately broke into tears as she explained her little dog's problem. "Doctor, something is terribly wrong with Little Fifi. I'm worried to death about her!"

As I looked at Little Fifi standing there on my exam table, eyes bright and alert, hair clean and shiny, and tail wagging to beat the band, I couldn't help but think that her owner was imagining things. With loving-kindness, I asked, "Mrs. T., what is it that makes you suspicious that something is wrong with Little Fifi?"

Without the slightest hesitation she answered, "Doctor, this morning when I let her outside to do her business, she only circled around twice before she pooped. Something is wrong, I just know it! She always, always, always spins around three times before she goes. Doctor, what's the matter with her?"

Standing there as she related this intimate tidbit of Little FiFi's medical history, I had to admit to myself that I had absolutely no idea of what was wrong. To the best of my recollection, neither I, nor any of my classmates for that matter, ever were taught anything about the infamous "not dancing before defecation" disease while we were in vet school. As I looked at the owner standing across the exam room table from me, her serious countenance and look of absolute concern assured me that she was not in the slightest bit putting me on. "Well," I said, "I'm not sure yet what Little FiFi's problem could possibly be, but let me just give her a good physical examination, and maybe I'll find something."

After a careful and very meticulous exam, the only abnormal finding I could discover was that the scent glands in Little FiFi's rear end were abnormally enlarged. I explained to Mrs. T. how, when these glands are overfull, they cause small dogs like Little FiFi a great deal of discomfort. This pain, in turn, leads to a reluctance to defecate. I then expressed (the medical term for emptying) the scent glands and gave Mrs. T. the prognosis that everything would be all right by morning. And sure enough, when I followed up the next day, Mrs. T., with the greatest relief, happily informed me that her sweet Little Fifi had performed the perfect number of pirouettes that morning before pooping, and all was again well. I really like owners like Mrs. T.

At the other end of the pet's health awareness spectrum, however, there are the owners who seem to be completely unconscious of the health needs and medical condition of their animal. Sadly, I see a lot of this type of owner as well.

Mr. W is an example of one of these. He's a good man, very intelligent, with a good job and beautiful family, but for reasons I'll never understand, he just plain doesn't pay any attention to his dog, Duke. I see Mr. W at the most once every three years when he brings in Duke for his rabies shot. I'm sure Mr. W wouldn't even do this much for his dog's health if it weren't for the multiple summonses he's received in the past, which force him to get Duke's license.

And poor old Duke, every time I see him, he just keeps looking worse and worse. Although he always appears well fed and in no way abused, his ears are always swollen and inflamed with a stinking, smelly yeast infection. He has fleas so bad that he has scratched all of the hair off of his back and around his tail-head. On both of his hind legs, the dewclaws, which should have been removed at birth, are so long that they've circled around and are now growing into themselves.

When I point out all of these facts to Mr. W, he pretends concern and then gives me some song-and-dance story about how he's tried all of these vinegar, alcohol, baking soda, or hydrogen peroxide home remedies on Duke's ears; he rambles on about how he's tried all of the store-bought flea sprays, powders, ointments, and drops there are in existence, and how nothing ever seems to work; and when I point out the severe infection in Duke's dewclaws, he just shrugs it off with some crap about how Duke, years ago, had bitten him while he tried to trim the dog's nails.

I asked him why he doesn't bring Duke in more regularly so I can help him take better care of the dog. His answer was just about what I suspected: "Nah, I never seem to have the time. Besides, Doc, he's just a damned dog." Sometimes you just have to wonder about people like Mr. W.

But as valuable as owners' perceptions and observations are, sometimes you have to take whatever information an owner may tell you regarding their pet's health history with a prudent amount of caution. Sometimes, either out of laziness, indifference, or just plain selfish desperation, some clients will stretch the truth—and some will lie outright—in order to get their desired result.

I'd never before seen the client who was now standing across the reception desk with her German shepherd, mixed-breed dog, Gracie. She was in my clinic to leave the dog for spaying. As we were filling out the paperwork, one of the first things that caught my attention was that she had come from a town about forty miles to the north of where my practice is located. Curious, I asked her why she had traveled so far with Gracie for such a routine procedure. She hit me with the vanity answer: "Oh Doctor, I've heard so much about how wonderful you are and how great you treat the animals." What could I say to that? I smiled and thanked her for her kind words.

After the paperwork was finished, we brought the dog into the exam room. I picked her up, placed her on the table, and began to do my usual presurgical physical examination. Gracie, according to her owner, was about four years old. As I examined her, the next thing that caught my attention was a question regarding the dog's vaccination status. When I asked the owner about the details, she said, "Oh, don't worry, Doctor, she's up to date. I think." When I pursued the question further, however, she admitted that she really wasn't sure of exactly when the last shots were given.

This answer is not uncommon; people lead busy lives, and it's hard to remember everything. I told her we'd better update her vaccinations, especially the dog's rabies shot. The tone in her voice and her quick, "OK, Doc, whatever you want to do," suggested to me the possibility that this might just be the first time in her whole life that Gracie had ever been to a vet.

No problem, she was here now, and I'd see to it she got her vaccinations.

The only other suspicion I had was that Gracie's belly seemed a little round and tight. "Oh, she's always had a big belly, Doctor. Don't worry about it, she just loves to eat." I could sense a slight tension in her voice but shrugged it off as her just being nervous. When I asked Gracie's owner about the possibility of pregnancy, she assured me that it was not possible. "She just went through her heat about two or three weeks ago. And besides that, she never *ever* goes outside." I stood there for a couple of minutes and thought about the situation some before I spoke.

In my mind, I kicked around a couple of possibilities for the dog's big belly. My first impression was that Gracie was pregnant. As a personal policy, I won't do a spay on a dog who's pregnant if I can avoid it. Not only do I have problems with it morally, but from a surgeon's point of view, the procedure can be a really sloppy mess.

But I reminded myself that Gracie's mom assured me that pregnancy wasn't possible. So I then thought maybe Gracie was, indeed, just a big chow hound and was just fat. I also kicked around a third possibility of her possibly having a serious medical problem in which pus and fluid accumulate in the dog's uterus. This sometimes fatal condition is called a pyometra. It could just be possible that the signs of heat her owner noticed a couple of weeks previously was a bloody discharge that could be the result from having a pyometra.

After these couple seconds of silent thought, I told her what I was thinking and suggested we do an X ray, just in case she had a pyometra or (and I was very careful how I mentioned this last possibility) just on the outside chance she may have missed seeing Gracie get pregnant. I could see a look of concern (panic?) and perhaps just a little bit of impatient irritation starting to work its way over her face. A split second later, without any hesitation whatsoever, she said, "No, I don't want her X-rayed! I just want her spayed."

I stood there for a couple more seconds and was about to tell her to take the dog somewhere else; I had the worst feeling that this dog was a disaster waiting to happen. But something told me to just go ahead and do it. I asked her one more time if it was at all possible the dog could have been bred, and she assured me pregnancy was not at all possible. And I believed her.

After saying good-bye to the owner, I then weighed sweet Gracie and gave her the injection that would anesthetize her. After she was sound asleep, I picked her up onto the surgery table and began prepping her for surgery. As I shaved around her teats, I examined them very closely to make sure there was no milk in them. There wasn't. Had there been, I'd have been sure of pregnancy and would have stopped then and there. When all was ready to proceed, I scrubbed, gloved up, and began Gracie's surgery.

I started the operation by making a routine two-inch-long incision on the midline of her abdomen just behind the belly button. And right off the bat, just as soon as I entered into her abdominal cavity, I realized that something was wrong. Instead of the small, pencil-sized, normal uterus I was expecting to find, there was this gigantic, fluid-filled organ about the size of two big rolls of bologna. "Son of a gun," I said to myself [those weren't the exact words I used], as I then tried to figure out what was going on. I wished, with all of my heart, that I'd insisted on doing an X ray. But it was too late now; whatever this thing was, it would now have to come out.

I found myself becoming a little bit irritated. Instead of the nice, neat, small incision I would normally have made during a routine spay, I would now have to increase the size of the opening to at least eight inches long in order to allow me to pull this gigantic uterus out of the poor dog's belly. As I began to do so, confused and conflicting thoughts went through my aggravated mind as I tried to decide what would be the best to do. Was this a pregnancy after all? There was no milk in her titties. Maybe she was just early in her term and therefore too early for the glands to form milk. Or was it possible that she had been pregnant but for some reason couldn't carry to term, and that these were just dead fetuses surrounded by fluid and pus? Maybe the signs of heat the owner saw was just a warning of a miscarriage. Maybe she did have a pyometra after all.

I was soon to have my answer. Whatever the problem was, it had caused the wall of her uterus to become as thin and fragile as a water-filled balloon. As I frantically struggled to keep control of this slippery, slimy glob of guts, a small section of it caught on the edge of one of the towel clamps that fastened the drape sheet to the dog, and it ruptured.

Now I had a real mess! Before I knew what in the heck had happened, a gallon or more of fluid burst forth from inside the uterus and spilled out all over me, the surgery table, and the floor. Anger at the owner (rage would be a better word) mixed with a near hysterical concern for the life of this poor dog consumed my entire being as I tried to figure out what to do next. I remember the first thing I did was holler to my wife (who was down in the next room working on the monthly reminder cards and had no idea of the carnage she was about to face), to please—Yes! I did say please—get up here and help me. Now!

There was nothing she could do to help with the surgery, but I thought that if she could at least clean up the floor where I was standing, I wouldn't slip and fall and break my neck. As she did so, I concentrated on getting the patient's surgery back under control. The rupturing of the uterus and the emptying of its fluid contents had one benefit: it at least made the organ easier to work with. After collecting my thoughts, I made the decision to continue the surgery by doing a complete ovario-hysterectomy; that is, I decided to completely remove both the ovaries and the uterus just as I would in a normal spay. So I gathered all of her internal body parts back up onto the surgical drape sheet and began the first step of removing the uterus by ligating (tying off) her ovaries.

I knew now that Gracie had been pregnant. But because I couldn't feel any movement in the several masses of tissue that still remained inside of the uterus, I concluded they were probably just dead pups. As I concentrated on the job at hand, my wife continued to quietly soak up and clean the gooey mess at my feet. She knew from experience not to bother me any more than she had to when I was in this state of high concentration and irritation.

She did, however, ask me what to do with a brown blob she'd found on the floor that had gushed out with the initial rupture. She held it up for me to look at, and I decided it was dead pup still in its birth sack. I told her to just go ahead and throw it in the wastebasket for now.

I then continued the surgery.

Several seconds passed, and I wondered why Theresa hadn't come back to finish cleaning up the floor—the squishing feeling under my feet was driving me crazy. I looked up to see her standing off to my right, perfectly still. She was intently gazing at the waste bin. "Theresa, please," I asked as calmly as I could in my desperate situation, "could you finish with the floor. I'm gonna slip and fall." There was no response.

A little agitated, I asked her again what was going on. She looked at me and said, "It looks like a normal puppy!" Apparently, as I was busy trying to gain the upper hand on the mess I was dealing with on my table, she had taken a second to break open the membrane of the blob of tissue she had picked up and discovered it was a puppy.

Now, a little bit annoyed, I told her again that it was probably dead, to just leave it be. I mentally reminded myself that because there was no milk in dog's mammary glands, and because the placenta didn't look quite right, it was probably just a premature, dead fetus. I reminded Theresa we now needed to concentrate all of our efforts on trying to save the mother.

There was absolute silence. As I watched her, I could tell by the painful expression on her face that she was grappling in her mind as to what to do. She knew I was dealing with a very serious situation, and I didn't need any additional aggravation. She knew I needed to pay attention to what I was doing. She knew I needed help, but she had something she needed to tell me. A little bit exasperated, I asked her again to just leave it.

She looked at me, the tears welling up in her eyes, and then looked back toward the wastebasket and cried out, "But Richard, *IT'S BREATHING!*"

"Ah poop" [again, not my exact word], I said, as I stopped for a second. I was now completely drained of all emotion. "You're not serious, are you?" But by the time I spoke, she'd already picked the little creature out of the garbage and was getting a towel and heat lamp ready. I walked over to where the little infant was lying, and sure enough, about every five or so seconds, the little guy would gasp out a tiny little breath. Without a single word from her, I now knew that, besides trying to save mama, we'd also have to try to save these little pups.

And so we did. Using the original rupture hole, I gently worked out, one by one, each of the babies from Gracie's uterus. After I milked each one out, I'd drop it into a waiting clean towel in Theresa's hands. She would then remove the birth membranes and cut off the umbilical cords. After successfully removing Gracie's six tiny puppies, I then returned to the job of completing her surgery.

An hour later, I had Gracie all sewed back together and in the recovery room cage. Theresa had all six pups, which ranged from beagle-looking to coonhoundish in appearance, dried off and under a heat lamp. She even already had a name for the critter she saved from the garbage: Rusty Chevrolet. We both were, however, still quite worried; even though they looked fine at that moment, because of them being born (I'm not sure *born* is the right word to use) premature, we both knew the chances of them living much longer were pretty slim.

There were also two other problems I now had to deal with. The first was what was I going to tell the owner. Theresa and I were now of the opinion that the lady's intention all along was to deceive me into spaying this dog that she knew good and well was pregnant. That's the reason she had traveled so far to my clinic for the surgery; she couldn't trick anyone else into doing it where she lived.

My quick assessment of her during our short office visit earlier that morning also gave me the impression that, even if she wanted to, she didn't have the skill, time, financial resources, or, most importantly, the necessary dedication to care for these infants. The biggest worry I had, however, was that, being the insensitive type of person that she was, the woman might just tell me to put the pups to sleep once she knew about them. After all of our effort to save these little guys, having to euthanize them would have pissed me off like crazy; but even more important, it would have just devastated Theresa.

The other problem I now faced was that if I said nothing, it would still leave the need of having to take care of the squirming and now hungry, still-very-much-alive tiny blessings that Theresa had under the heat lamp. Their mother had no milk for them, which meant that if they lived, Theresa—or someone—would have to feed them at least six times a day.

And so, when everything was finished, I sat down with Theresa, and we tried to decide what to do. We both agreed that if the owner was told about the pups, she would flatly refuse to take them home. Even worse, we were afraid she would probably insist we put them to sleep. I also asked several close friends and colleagues what their thoughts were regarding the ethics and morality of the whole situation; one response was consistent throughout every conversation we had: Don't tell the owner about the pups.

When evening office hours came around and Gracie's mother stopped by to pick her up, I told her—as straight-faced as I could—that, with the exception of the dog being pregnant, everything went well with the surgery. I might just as well have been talking to a wall.

"I don't owe you anything extra. Do I?" was all she said. She couldn't have cared less about Gracie's surgery or what might have happened to the puppies, which was good for me. Technically, I'd told her the whole truth, and now I was in the clear. I concluded our transaction by telling her she didn't owe me any more money, that the dog's stitches had to be removed in two weeks, and then I thanked her for driving all the way down from up north to see me.

The pups, by some strange fortune, all lived, and still live to this very day. We phoned an absolute saint of a lady friend of ours, Barb, and asked her if she'd be interested in caring for these pups. In a New York minute, she said yes. I warned her over and over again that the chore could very likely turn out to be a heartbreak, because there was a good chance that as soon as the pups' baby fat was gone, they might not make it. She insisted on trying anyway and took them home. When I called to check on them the next morning, she said all six were still alive. I told her it was a miracle.

A couple of weeks later, I called Gracie's mom to remind her about removing the stitches. She snarled at the intrusion. She said she got a nurse friend of hers to remove them and then hung up. I've never seen her since.

Barb, unbelievably, managed to save every single pup. She found loving homes for all but one, and this was only because she wanted him for herself. And ironically, the one she liked the best was the same one Theresa rescued from the trash can, little Rusty Chevrolet.

Chapter Fifteen

The Eternal Bond

On the southeast corner of the Caribbean land of Aruba, there's a windswept patch of grass- and vine-covered sand dunes, about an acre in size, known simply as The Animal Cemetery. My wife and I visited the spot on our last vacation to the country, and it was a very moving sight.

It is here on this beautiful little plot of oceanside beach that the loving pet owners who live on this happy island come to lay to eternal rest their cherished pets. Inscribed on the hundreds of simple wooden crosses and grave markers are names like Ladre, Touckey, Erica, Fiel, Dun Dun, and Argento; also, on many of these markers, written in either Papiamento (the local language of the island of Aruba) or in Dutch, is the grieving owner's last good-bye to their departed friends. Lovingly placed at the base of many of these markers is a pet's favorite toy or a simple bouquet of plastic flowers.

On one of the highest grassy promontories within the ancient walls of Scotland's famous Edinburgh Castle, in a position of high honor, lie in eternal rest the bodies of British military units' mascots, both dogs and cats, from over the last five centuries, who had distinguished themselves or had fallen in battle during their nation's seemingly endless wars or military campaigns.

In the early 1970s, just outside of the Chinese city of Wuhan, a group of soldiers noticed that the soil upon which they were camped was a different color from that of the brick-red clay they were used to seeing. When a government archaeologist arrived on the scene to investigate, they discovered that the soldiers had actually stumbled upon a huge, undisturbed, 2,400-year-old tomb. The Chinese government then painstakingly collected all of the artifacts from the tomb and built an excellent, people-friendly museum (which my wife and I visited) to display and preserve them.

The museum's collection includes the coffin and remains of Marquis Yi of Zeng (the tomb's owner), the coffins and remains of his eight concubines (quite a frisky guy, the old marquis), and his thirteen servants, all of whom had the dubious honor of being buried with their master.

In addition to the Marquis Yi, his eight concubines, and lucky thirteen servants, there was one additional small coffin located in the position of highest honor at the marquis's feet. Was it his be-loved wife? Nope! My personal feeling is that with eight concubines, I don't see how the old marquis could have had time for a wife. The coffin contained the remains of his most-treasured dog, placed at his feet, just as he was in life, to protect him and his family in their eternal sleep.

In an old college textbook of Greek literature, which sits among the hundreds of books on my library shelf, is this poem, written in 400 B.C. by an unknown author:

Stranger by the roadside, do not smile

When you see this grave, though it is only a dog's.

My master wept when I died, and his own hand

Laid me in the earth and wrote these lines on my tomb.

(*Antæus: Literature As Pleasure.*

Daniel Halpern, editor)

In an old *National Geographic* (and I'm sorry I don't know which one; I had torn out the picture so I wouldn't lose it, but did so anyway) there was a photograph of a 10,000- year-old dog burial site, located somewhere in southern Europe. Careful excavation by archaeologists revealed that the dog had been tenderly placed into the ground with flowers, food, and a few wooden objects, again, probably his or her favorite toys.

As the above five examples illustrate, the expression of grief at the loss of one's treasured pet is as boundless and universal, in both time and space, as that of the sense of loss suffered by the passing on of a fellow human being. Just the hundreds of examples I've seen in my practice alone of the anguish and pain people undergo at the loss of their pet would take me weeks to describe. This sense of grief has always greatly moved me, and I often wonder (in my relatively few moments of quiet reflection) just why it is that people grieve so very much the loss of a treasured pet.

Books I've read on the subject of pet loss have one, or both, of the following explanations for this intense feeling we experience when a pet dies. The first says that in a span of fifteen or so years (barring any accidents), we're blessed with the opportunity to watch our dog or cat grow from the rambunctious and inexhaustible energy of youth, into a mature and confident adult, and, if we're lucky, then on to a dignified, peaceful old age. And just when it seems that we finally get to *really* know them, they're taken away from us.

A second reason these books say we feel such loss is because our pet's love for us is an absolute and totally nonjudgmental form of love; they love us if we're happy, and they love us if we're miserable. I've heard it said a hundred times, that when you get right down to it, our pets usually have all of the trustworthy and loyal qualities we wish we could find in our best friends.

These are good reasons, and I agree wholeheartedly with their logic. But I think the answer is far, far deeper than these explanations would lead us to believe. I think the sense of loss has more to do with the nature of the bond that loving dog and cat owners must form with their pets. It all has to do with the way we have to communicate with each other.

I personally feel that because our cats or dogs can't talk with their owners in precise words like our fellow humans can, they must then communicate with us on a level far higher than that simply of speaking and listening. If we want to truly understand our pet's needs and wants, we're forced to pay closer attention to each other; we must be especially sensitive to the subtle details: facial expressions, body language, and behaviors. We almost have to be able to read each others' minds.

Without sounding too New Age, I think it is because of this deeper level of communication and bonding that occurs between us and our pets that we grieve so when a beloved pet dies. For an all too short period of time, we establish such a powerful cosmic connection with one another, that when this bond is broken, and they are snatched away from us by death, a large part of us dies with them as well.

EPILOGUE

A couple of years ago, I was working on the roof of a new pole barn I was building down the road from my home. As I was nailing down some two-by-fours up near the peak of the roof, I happened to look out over at my wife's sheep pasture, and my eye caught a glance of a little white blur that was trailing behind one of the peacefully grazing sheep. I said to myself, "Richard, that looks like a little lamb out there behind that sheep." After thinking about it some, I answered myself, "Nah, it can't be; we didn't let the ram in with them yet this year." (For those who may not know, a ram is a male sheep.)

But just to make sure, I climbed down from the roof, clambered over the fence, and walked out into the pasture. And sure enough, there was Old Flo, and she did indeed have herself a little baby. After a couple of minutes of chasing the little darling (it's amazing how those little newborn lambs can run), I finally caught it. After looking her over and satisfying myself that she was healthy, I let her go. She instantly ran back lickety-split to her anxiously waiting mother, and started to nurse.

I watched them both for a couple of minutes to make sure everything was going to be all right before starting to walk back to my building project. But as I was walking, I stopped, and for no particular reason, turned around to look one more time at the mama sheep and her baby. Old Flo was still standing there contentedly chewing her cud, as her little lamb continued to nurse away with great enthusiasm. I found myself wondering again how in the heck she could have gotten pregnant. Also, I thought, *Why her? She's so old.*

The only thing I could think of was that Skippy, our ram, probably under the intoxicating influence of one of our sunny, upstate New York springtime days, must have jumped the fence, had a romantic rendezvous with his old girlfriend, found himself gratified by the encounter, and then jumped back into his own pasture.

Then, as I am frequently prone to do, I drifted off and began thinking about the greater picture. I thought about how determined and magnificent this fragile force is that we call life; of how full of wonders—some heartbreaking, but most full of joy and awe—our universe is; of how the natural order of things—birth, living, and death—could probably all be summed up in a single moment by simply watching Old Flo feeding her newborn lamb on that beautiful summer morning. And I think it's all quite wonderful. Thank you.